The Conservative's Dilemma

By

Robert Villegas

The Conservative's Dilemma

By Robert Villegas.

Published in the USA

Updated 10/22/2019

ISBN-13: 978-1523416431

ISBN-10: 1523416432

Library of Congress Control Number 2016903660

www.robertvillegas.com

Series Title: Villegas Politics Volume 5

Table of Contents

Introduction

I wrote this book to ask some important questions:

1. Will we become again a free people, deciding as individuals the direction of our lives or will we continue to be herded into groups and classes to be favored or rejected by a ruling elite?
2. Will we be free to start businesses, earn profits and keep those profits or will we be enslaved in order to feed the government as it advances social engineering and corporatist (cronyist) schemes?
3. Will we pay high taxes or low taxes?
4. Will we be allowed to participate in our own lives or be mindless slaves to the wishes of others?
5. Will we trust our government to defend our rights or fear our government for its high handed practices, its coercion, its ever-changing decrees?
6. Will our money be strong and purchase a large array of fine products to improve our lives or will it be stolen and put into the coffers of financial thieves in the treasury and Cayman Islands?
7. Who are the villains today; the hard working people who want better lives and enjoyment or the government that wants us to sacrifice for the sake of those who have no desire to work?
8. Will we be a society of people who earn money through production or through standing in protest lines to further government re-distribution?
9. And finally, will the conservatives save our country from dictatorship and decline?

I think it is important that hard working citizens learn the real issues that affect our lives and take definitive action when we think the government is stepping out of bounds. The Constitution, as it was originally written, does not allow the government to violate the rights of citizens. When pork-filled government programs are created without discussion or approval by the people, when government passes laws without debate, creates programs without justification, spends money that does not exist, then it must be stopped by responsible dissent. Such dissent is the continuation of the American Revolution.

Today, we are being led by two basic groups of politicians. The progressive Democrats who foster government coercion and the conservative Republicans who help them. Both groups foster government power but from a slightly different perspective; one group would like to rule our actions "for our own good" while the other would like to see a little less government force and some free market elements. The result is compromise favoring the advance toward totalitarianism.

Among conservatives there are five distinct groups.
- The neocons include intellectuals and politicians who are actually progressives seeking to beat the progressives to their spending programs.
- The evangelicals want to legislate private morality.
- Economic conservatives adhere to a regulated capitalist system ripe with cronyism and corporate welfare.

- Constitutionalists or Tea Party members want to return to constitutional liberties through the Bill of Rights.
- Libertarians base their philosophy upon thinkers such as Murray Rothbard and Harry Browne and also function as a separate political party. Their goal is anarcho-capitalism, a mongrel form of capitalism that would self-destruct through the elimination of all governments.

None of these five groups dominates the Republican Party. They all, in a sense, need each other because none of them can win elections without compromise with one or more of the other groups.

These groups have tried to work together to win elections but there have been few elections won and the association of one group with one of the others has served, in some cases, to discredit them with independent and progressive voters.

For instance, the neocons need the support of the economic conservatives who have traditionally supported them until recently (now that the neocons are seen more as progressives rather than conservatives). Lately, the Tea Party faction can no longer be counted upon to support neocons and economic conservatives because the neocons have been exposed as supporting liberal policies including cronyism. The Tea Party has convinced many Republicans and independents that the neocons and economic conservatives will always vote with the progressives and abandon individual rights[1] at almost every turn. In fact, many Tea Partiers insinuate that individual rights should be what conservatives should stand for while many of them are actually closet evangelicals seeking a theocracy.

Additionally, many economic conservatives have grown weary of the evangelicals because of their penchant to ignore individual rights when it comes to freedom of speech and a woman's right to abortion. The evangelicals have proven themselves to be openly for theocracy rather than for a republican form of government and many rights-respecting conservatives fear that the evangelicals will push for theocracy and bans on abortion. Likewise, the evangelicals have put the Republican Party on notice that unless their issues are addressed they will stay home.

How can these disparate groups bridge their differences and win elections? Judging from the large numbers of conservatives who stayed home in 2012 something has to change. At the very least, some conservatives will have to drop their deep-seated premises in order to win elections and that is a non-starter for many of them. They would prefer to *appear* to be working together so that they can dominate later after electoral victory.

---

[1] The principle that the individual is the locus of virtue; that all decisions should be made by the individual for the individual and no one has a right to interfere with the individual's rights to life, liberty and happiness. It also holds that the only role of government is to protect individual rights and not violate them. The purpose of the Bill of Rights in our Constitution is to spell out, in as much specificity as possible, what those rights are as well as how rights not enumerated in the Constitution should be protected.

The result of this "unholy" alliance is a weak electoral effort and many lost elections. In this book, I will discuss the major issues that affect the conservative movement and attempt to make some sense of the Conservative's dilemma.

The Forgotten "ism"

During the late 1930s of the last century our political discourse was hijacked and many commonly understood words were changed to mush; it was during this time that we forgot one of our most important "isms".

In fact, this forgotten "ism" has a distinguished, benevolent past. At one time, it was the foundation for one of the greatest transformations in world history; a transformation that changed the face of the earth for the better. This "ism", once forgotten, became buried under volumes of obfuscation and misrepresentation. It was deliberately hidden from us by men who wanted us to forget that it was once our salvation. Indeed, our "forgetting" it has brought about one of the tragedies of history. This forgotten "ism" was fathered by the Enlightenment.

As Isaac Kramnick describes it:

"...political differences notwithstanding, the intellectuals of the French and British Enlightenment operated in relatively similar settings. They shared the profound transformation of Western life brought by commerce and industrialization and, with it, the emergence of middle-class Figaros (as in Mozart's opera Le marriage de Figaro) as the new cultural ideal. Far from being alarmed at this great change, they generally embraced the new commercial civilization and its values, seeing it as a progressive, reforming force that would undermine the dead hand of aristocratic privilege and religious fanaticism. Theirs was also an age of increasing literacy, as for the first time in history reading ceased to be a monopoly of the very few, the rich, and the clergy. It was also an age when intellectuals eagerly wrote for and to this wider audience of new readers, not yet having become alienated from the philistine public in a posture of romantic weariness. (parentheses mine)

"What was the message of these Enlightenment intellectuals? What were their ideals? They believed that unassisted human reason, not faith or tradition, was the principal guide to human conduct...Particularly suspect was religious faith and superstition. Humanity was not innately corrupt as Catholicism taught, nor was the good life found only in a beatific state of otherworldly salvation. Pleasure and happiness were worthy ends of life and realizable in this world. The natural universe, governed not by miraculous whimsy of a supernatural God, was ruled by rational scientific laws, which were accessible to human beings through the scientific method of experiment and empirical observation. Science and technology were the engines of progress enabling modern men and women to force nature to serve their well-being and further their happiness. Science and the conquest of superstition and ignorance provided the prospect for endless improvement and reformation of the human condition, progress even unto a future that was perfection. The Enlightenment valorized the individual and the moral legitimacy of self-interest. It sought to free the individual from all varieties of external corporate or communal constraints, and it sought to reorganize the political, moral intellectual, and economic worlds to serve individual interest."[2]

Philosopher John Locke taught "…(t)hat individual mind imperially ordered chaotic sensory experience, constructing, therefore, its own meaning for the world. This Lockean portrayal of individuals as sole intellectual creators of their universe dominates the eighteenth century, from the writings of his disciples Hartley and Condillac to Helvètius, Beccaria, and Condorcet. No wonder, then, that Diderot and d'Alembert dedicated the Encyclopeie in part to Locke.

"It wasn't only Locke's Essay on Human Understanding, however, that held the Enlightenment in thrall. It was also the political liberalism of his Second Treatise on Civil Government. Indeed, it is in its basic assumptions about society, so heavily influenced by Locke, that one sees best the linkage of the Enlightenment's ideals and liberal individualism. Enlightenment liberalism set the individual free politically, intellectually and economically. The political universe was demystified, as the magical power of thrones, scepters, and crowns was replaced by rational acts of consent. The individual (understood, of course, in the Enlightenment as male and property-owning) did not receive government and authority from a God who had given his secular sword to princes and magistrates to rule by his divine right. Nor did the individual keep any longer to his subordinate place in a divinely inspired hierarchy, in

---

[2] The Portable Enlightenment Reader, edited by Isaac Kramnick, paperback, The Viking Portable Library

which kings and noblemen had been placed above him as "your highnesses" who were society's natural governors. Government was voluntarily established by free individuals through a willful act of contract. Individuals rationally consented to limit their own freedom and to obey civil authority in order to have public protection of their natural rights. Government's purpose was to serve self-interest, to enable individuals to enjoy peacefully their rights to life, liberty, and property, not to serve the glory of God or dynasties, and certainly not to dictate moral or religious truth."[3]

Condorcet:

"The time will therefore come when the sun will shine only on free men who know no other master but their reason; when tyrants and slaves, priests and their stupid or hypocritical instruments will exist only in the works of history and on the stage; and when we shall think of them only to pity their victims and their dupes; to maintain ourselves in a state of vigilance by thinking on their excesses; and to learn how to recognize and so to destroy, by force of reason, the first seeds of tyranny and superstition, should they ever dare to reappear amongst us."[4]

If you want to see what makes the United States different

---

[3] The Future Progress of the Human Mind, Marquis de Condorcet (1743-1794) Reprinted in The Portable Enlightenment Reader edited by Isaac Kramnick, the Viking Portable Library
[4] *Esquisse d'un tableau historique des progrès de l'esprit humain* (Sketch for a historical picture of the progress of the human mind)

from any other nation, don't assume it is because we are a Christian nation. Instead, look at the whole history of philosophy and recognize the magnificent transformation that was created by the Enlightenment and by the secularism that it inaugurated. Indeed, the Enlightenment and the Constitution of the U.S. both sought to mitigate the problems inherent in theocracy and dictatorship (based, at the time upon the tyranny of the King of England who also headed the state religion).

The philosophical movement called the Enlightenment resulted in a totally new age that spawned the scientific method, individual rights, limited government, economic freedom, the separation of church and state – and most importantly the right to happiness. These ideas liberated the individual mind and taught man to think and do as he willed, to travel, to learn about the world and to decide for himself the answers to the major questions of the ages. These ideas, not faith, are the cause of decades of affluence; the societies that institute them are the best, cleanest and safest in the world today.

Organized religion did not bring the ideas of the Enlightenment to the world but instead fought them for centuries. Before the Enlightenment gained influence, religion brought us oppression and political domination in the name of God. Although we seldom hear stories about the Inquisition and its tortures, we are often told that such oppressive practices were rare, exceptions to the norm, etc. But were they really rare? Consider the patristic view of sex that still animates religion. Sexual freedom, homosexuality, abortion, marriage laws and the fear of individuality dominate religious groups today. Taylor informs us:

"Just as in the past, patrists do not merely condemn sexual freedom as immoral, they also assert that it is destructive to society. For instance, in 1935, Canon Bickersteth wrote to *The Times,* apparently in complete seriousness, to say, "The increase in adultery and the breaking of the marriage laws are greater dangers to national safety than bombing from the air." (Similarly, in the first World War, French army chaplains attributed military reverses to sexual promiscuity, just as, more than two millennia previously, the Israelites attributed their defeat by the Philistines to the same cause.) Historically, of course, this is a ridiculous claim: as we have seen, periods such as the Renaissance and the eighteenth century, which were periods of unusual sexual freedom, were periods of great achievement and expansion. What the patrist means in making this claim is not that a permissive code will destroy society, but that it will destroy the sort of society he desires."[5] We could, of course, point to contemporary conservative patrists who claim that natural disasters and terrorism are God's punishment over sexual freedom and homosexuality. There is no better way to discredit your political views than by offering moral pronouncements such as the above for the media to disseminate around the world.

---

[5] Sex in History by G. Rattray Taylor, Harper Torchbooks, Page 299

Yet, I think the best way to understand our Enlightenment society is to analyze how the Constitution bans religion in the First Amendment and especially why the Founders chose to do so. To quote:

"Congress shall make no law respecting an establishment of religion, or prohibiting the free exercise thereof; or abridging the freedom of speech, or of the press, or the right of the people peaceably to assemble, and to petition the Government for a redress of grievances."[6]

Yet, the first phrase says that the government cannot establish a religion or enact a law that establishes a state religion over the people. If this is not a direct prohibition of religion in public life, I don't know what is. Why did the Founders insist on this Amendment? Because they knew that people had differing views on many topics and especially religion. They knew of the many religious conflicts where one group sought to impose itself (through war or legislation) on other groups. They knew the history of Christianity and the utter disregard it has had for people that sought to think differently. They knew of Galileo's struggles and other thinkers who were punished and ostracized for disagreeing with the Church. They knew about the Inquisition and the witch trials. They also knew that many people came to the American continent specifically to escape religious persecution in Europe and elsewhere. They knew that the best way to ensure that people could think for themselves as free

---

[6] The Bill of Rights

people was to ensure that no one religion got control of the government. So they specifically prohibited the establishment of religion by government.

Notice they did not prohibit religion as long as it was practiced privately and through the consent of people who accepted its tenets. In fact, the second phrase about not prohibiting the free exercise of religion was intended to establish the prohibition of religion in a different way by protecting the free exercise of philosophical or religious ideas. In fact, the Constitution protects the mind against being forced to think in any way prescribed by others. Because of this phrase, people no longer saw the members of other religions as fearful or threatening. This situation did not exist before our Constitution.

Carry this idea further to the next phrase in the Constitution where the government could not prohibit free speech, or of the press, or the right of the people peaceably to assemble and you are on your way to creating a truly secular society by means of general principles that protect the mind and reason. The result of this protection is that people could be safe from persecution and prosecution for their ideas and beliefs – of any type. The benefits of free inquiry, open discussion and even the freedom to disagree with others all came from this Amendment and from the establishment of a government that protected the mind against coercion. This meant that any individual could, if he wanted, focus all attention on God as he understood him, or he could instead focus his attention on reality.

With the establishment of the Constitution, not only were people free of persecution for thinking, they were also free to develop new ideas and to express them. This created a free market of ideas where people could openly decide, without fear, what they thought. The result was better ideas, more useful ideas and this spurred the development of new products in an open market. Industries such as publishing, manufacturing, even political debates and strong disagreements could all flourish out in the open instead of in hidden backrooms. After a time, the result of free speech and free inquiry was a society that grew safer, citizens that grew more self-confident and an economy that grew stronger because the products being offered and delivered were increasingly better.

The last part of this Amendment, about petitioning the Government for a redress of grievances, established the basis for the judicial system where objective laws could settle disputes, where the government was the protector of rights and people dedicated to justice could actually dispense such justice in an impartial way. The focus of government was to ensure that no one had the right to appeal to and impose any ideas on the citizenry without coming up against a judicial protector of individual rights.

The First Amendment established the right of the free mind to live in society without threat or force. In essence, it established individual rights and liberated, above all, the previously captive mind. By outlawing religious domination, the American system of government inaugurated, for the first time on earth, or at least since the Greeks, a society where people were free to think, to speak their minds, to pursue economic wellbeing, to be safe and to live among other men with little fear of envy or robbery. This was the legacy of the Enlightenment: that the modern-day Socrates will not be forced to drink the hemlock.

Because of the Constitution, individualism became so strong in America that people (religious and non-religious) learned to think for themselves about what would make a better life. This meant that religion, rather than trying to secure its dominance as it did in Europe, had to accept a position of political powerlessness. This led to the establishment of capitalism and even to a nation of the most generous people in the world. Rather than having to live with a religion imposed by government, the separation of church and state forced religious altruists to merely exhort people to be altruistic and go to church. The newly rich and affluent people that built America, because freedom had made them affluent, became benevolent givers through voluntary contributions – they called it altruism, but this benevolence was expressed, not as altruism, but as generosity.

So what happened? What went wrong? What the history books seldom tell us is that, because of the Enlightenment, our new nation was the first to effectively liberate the mind of man, to establish reason as the method among men for dealing with each other. Generally speaking, as time went by, those who advocated reason, freedom, capitalism, individual rights and limited government were called "liberals". Their philosophy was called "liberalism" because they advocated "liberty".

What happened? The big mistake came when we dropped the emphasis on liberty and reason and started seeing our dueling "isms" as a conflict between religious conservatism and "secular" progressivism. This was the wrong fork in the road.

Conservatism

How is it that God and religion were once the agents of monarchy and state religion (the agents of the divine right of kings and the "off with his head" form of justice), while also being the agents of freedom and individual rights? Logically, the contradiction cannot be resolved and it points to the flaws inherent in the idea that our nation was a product of faith and God.

In Europe, as the Enlightenment flourished and began changing the world, many philosophers, because they were afraid that religion would die, did their best to undo the influence of reason. Kant and a number of other thinkers sought to save God and religion from the onslaught of science. In the name of reason, they declared that reason could not understand reality; they declared that man's sensory make up was not able to apprehend it. They split man's mind by giving it two options. One, that man could not understand reality because his sensory mechanism was incapable of seeing it as it was, and two, that true reality was created by the structure of man's (or God's) mind.

Even some of the leaders of the Enlightenment had difficulty reconciling a belief in God with the idea of reason. Deists, for example, attempted a compromise by declaring that God is the Creator of the universe but He no longer participates in historical events. This view was intended to make room for reason but it too relied on rationalism; it postulated a belief (in God) as the foundation for reality. When the choice for man is between two forms of rationalism (Theism and Deism), reason has no defenders among philosophers. Its influence must decline.

With few real defenders, the attacks against reason grew. Many thinkers, following Kant, argued that only religious morality could save man from being his own destroyer. The view that man is imperfect, with Kant's help, as well as the similar views of earlier "conservative" philosophers like Hobbes, survived the Enlightenment and gave the modern conservative movement the ammunition it needed to argue that the separation clause was never intended to eliminate religion in government; rather God and his commandments were necessary in order to save man from the sins of "imperfect" individuals.

Progressives, as their philosophy developed, saw government as the vehicle to accomplish God's plan for the victims of greed while conservatives moved toward religiously-based institutions (including government) to control man's greed. According to this view, religion was relevant because it was the only antidote to immorality. And by selectively focusing on certain aspects of Judeo-Christian theocracy, they argued that a free society was an outgrowth of societies described in the Bible.

Fundamentally, conservatives do not hold that reason is good for man. They hold that faith in God is superior to reason, that God is the ruler of the universe and men should be subservient to God's plan. This is decidedly not the same philosophy that influenced many of the Founders when they declared that man had the right to the pursuit of happiness.

The pattern of the conservative strategy (that would also emerge in the progressive strategy) has been to change the meanings of terms presented in the Enlightenment-generated Constitution. The goal was to establish "sacrifice" as a defining motive of the Founders against the Constitutional protections of life, liberty and the pursuit of happiness; they preached against individualism and demanded that both the church and government follow God's view of what was right for men. They sought to undermine a woman's right to her body by claiming to be against "murder" of babies. They fought against the teachings of science in the schools, especially the scientifically proven views of Darwin and his theory of evolution. They advanced a literal interpretation of myths found in the Bible. They argued about the Pledge of Allegiance, into which they had inserted the words "under

God", and about removing God from our schools, Christmas decorations, even efforts to secularize Christmas (which had a secular past as well). They accused the progressives and other secularists of being atheists who hated God. They sought to ostracize and disenfranchise these people in order to defeat opposition to their own growing incursions, and, in an effort to enter the mainstream of political thought, they never mentioned that their actual goal was theocracy.

The genesis of the conservative movement was a need to discredit the Enlightenment for its contribution to freedom. By claiming that only religion could successfully lead to a moral life and freedom, they strove to disconnect the Enlightenment from its influence as a moral force. They also strove to distort the individualism found in the Enlightenment (that consisted of men dedicated to reason rather than faith) by making a straw man out of secularism. They sought to bury the Enlightenment's cry for freedom by declaring it an agent of tyranny when, in fact, secularism was an outgrowth of the historically accurate truth that organized religion (and theocracy) was tyranny.

Through this twist of thinking, religion was able to associate itself with the good; creating a new movement of "freedom-loving" people who saw the rights developed in the Enlightenment as a gift from God, not part of man's nature. And to "prove" their point, they reminded us that the Declaration of Independence itself had said that rights were "endowed by their Creator". By taking the

Declaration out of the historical context of the Enlightenment, they transformed our founding principles to those of the very religion against which the Founders were attempting to rebel.

What they ignored is that the term "endowed by their Creator" was intended to be inclusive of all opinions about the source of rights especially "natural law" and Deism. And, since the Declaration was a statement of individual rights, the term "their Creator" did not mean that man belonged to God but that each person's interpretation of God was his own. Certainly, some of our founders believed that the Christian God was the source of rights and this position, to their minds, was consistent with the idea that God was nature. Yet, the Declaration made no mention of the Bible, Moses or supernatural intervention into the lives of men. Nor did it claim that man could only be moral by practicing God's injunctions. The intent of the Framers of the Declaration, rightly or wrongly, was to accommodate the views of all while also adhering to the principle that rights were derived from the laws of nature...from man's nature. This view was more consistent with Francis Bacon's view that "nature to be commanded must be obeyed" and that proper government must recognize that man must be free of any encroachment, religious or otherwise. The implication was not that rights were a gift from God but that they were derived from nature...regardless of how you interpreted nature.

But we must look at the Constitution to determine what

the Founders were trying to accomplish: "We the People of the United States, in Order to form a more perfect Union, establish Justice, insure domestic Tranquility, provide for the common defence, promote the general Welfare, and secure the Blessings of Liberty to ourselves and our Posterity, do ordain and establish this Constitution for the United States of America." Notice they did not say anything about religion when setting down the purpose of the document.

As the conservative movement grew, the Enlightenment philosophy that defended the individual, and made our nation possible, was now conveniently out of mind. When the progressives entered the fray and began to undo Constitutional protections, conservatives saw their opportunity to bury the influence of reason forever by connecting it to progressivism and government intrusions. Picking up on Marx's materialist views, that touted the value of logic over faith, and the communists' long-standing anti-religious persecutions, conservatives decided that if communists and socialists were advocates of science, then science, because it was this-worldly and materialistic, must also be false. They rejected the validity of science because this position enabled them to preach creationism. When comparing science with faith, they extolled the value of faith. When comparing materialism to spiritualism, they extolled the superiority of the spiritual and they praised the idea that there was a relationship of the spiritual with the free. In other words, the spirit is free.

This enabled the progressives to pick up the mantle of reason and science and gave prospective dictators the advantage. Rather than connect science with reality and an improving life for all, science became the handmaiden of dictatorship. When the progressives declared that they were advocates of reason, how could the advocates of rationalism and faith argue? Since Marx was not really scientific, neither were the progressives. Out goes reality for the conservatives and in comes pseudo-science for the progressives; the effort to use "logic" (that they called "science") to validate government power and collectivism.

The arguments for capitalism as developed by Smith, Locke, classical economists and other "liberals" could now be used, in a distorted sense, to provide cover for the religious conservatives in times when they were out of power. For the conservatives, "free market" ideas helped create political outrage against the dishonesty of progressives. But the progressives and the universities were not listening.

Indeed, it is conservatives, in various forms, who have championed some of our most disastrous policies including Anti-trust, government regulations and political graft to name a few. In an effort to capitalize on the political success of the progressive movement they attempted to beat the progressives to entitlement programs and, most often, because they have no argument against altruism, they wound up "me-tooing" the progressives.

Conservative intellectuals and politicians use a religious, utilitarian, form of pro-capitalist argument in order to get into the mainstream of debate but, once in power, they ignore economic freedom in favor of establishing religion in society. The idea of "compassionate conservatism" that ignores the free market in favor of faith-based charity is nothing more than religious progressivism.

If you doubt my assessment of religious conservatives, consider that most evangelicals do not fight for individual rights. Their version of the fundamental unit in society is not the individual but the family. This form of collectivism holds that the family is the most important unit that must be protected in society. They use all sorts of "social" arguments that blame the family breakdown on selfishness and anti-social behavior. They claim that this breakdown causes crime, immorality, familial dysfunction and other "problems". By ignoring the value of the individual in society, they ignore his need to be free and proceed to enslave him or her to the family. They insist that self-sacrifice is the essence of our social strength. The progressives could not agree more. And since collectivism always requires a scapegoat, these conservatives are quick to blame the independence fostered by capitalism as the cause of society's breakdown. Their solution is more Anti-trust prosecutions and regulations. This leaves the door open for the progressives to "create" problems that can be blamed by both progressives and conservatives on capitalism.

Progressivism

Progressives, on the other hand, influenced by many of the same European philosophies as the conservatives, rather than seeking to establish religion, seek to use a more virulent form of collectivism as a cover for plunder. Their "god" is society; their ideas, also accepted on faith, pray to a different deity of power politics. Because of their Marxist base, they see their goal as gaining control of the "machines" and the factories so they can plunder production.

The influence of Kant and his philosophical descendants continued to grow in Europe even while the Enlightenment flowered in America. The power and influence of Hegel, Kant, Popper and others continued to feed the rhetoric of aspiring dictators. The progressive movement emigrated from Europe and became the American brand of communists, union organizers, socialists, pragmatists and today's progressives that are bent on expanding government through higher taxes and entitlement programs – an American form of a fascist state. Progressives make up a descending scale, a "slippery slope", so to speak. At the top of the slope are those that hide their true intentions by covering themselves as Constitutionalists who use the language of freedom. Sometimes we call these people "honest liberals". The more brazen, the bottom of the slope, admit they favor a violent overthrow of capitalism. I call them the "Alinsky Radicals". In essence, they are all the same; their only difference is the amount of force they claim to advocate. They all advocate force against citizens – this is the characteristic that invalidates their philosophy and exposes the lie that they are Constitutionalists.

History has shown that progressives will appropriate to themselves the language and emotions of their most powerful enemies in order to masquerade as people holding similar values. The early example was Kant himself. After declaring himself a man of the Enlightenment dedicated to reason, he maliciously wrote volumes to show men that there was no connection between man's mind and reality and that the only thing one could do is his duty to God.[7] Other thinkers such as Marx took these leads and provided the foundations for some of the most corrupt and murderous political systems in history, the various political 'isms' that required government brutality in order to accomplish feigned "social justice". The legacy of Kant and progressivism are millions of dead bodies.

In America, because of the Constitution, progressives had a different challenge. The Marxists and socialists tried at first to declare violent revolutions through labor unions. They attacked and denigrated capitalist leaders, calling them robbers, thieves, charlatans and crooks. As they changed colors and morphed into progressives, they did everything they could to pry the Constitution from the hands of the people so they could replace it with the same destructive systems through which their brothers

---

[7] What is Enlightenment? Immanuel Kant

had devastated Europe. That pesky Constitution has always been in the way.

In those early times they recognized the true enemy; reason and capitalism; while the emerging religious right had realized that their mortal enemy was the liberalism of the Enlightenment, the philosophy of reason and the individual.

In our early days, the two divisions of political thought were individualism/laissez faire capitalism (otherwise known as classical liberalism) and collectivism as embodied in the populists and early progressives such as Teddy Roosevelt. The classical liberals, who had nothing in common with today's liberals, were the embodiment of the Enlightenment that created our society, while the early progressives saw capitalism, self-interest and individualism as the problem, not because it did not work, it clearly was successful, but because capitalists stood in the way of their taking over the machines. The major fallacy of the classical liberals was that they chose to defend capitalism using the idea of praxeology and statistics. In other words, capitalism was not good because it was moral; it was good because it worked. The end result for both praxeology and progressivism is that they both defended "the common good". Because of Kant, they had nowhere else to go.

Progressives have sought to turn government from one that protects individuals to one that would coerce men into working for "social goals" or "social justice" as defined by them. They needed a scapegoat which they found in capitalism, an economic system that was nothing more than freedom. They turned capitalism into a pariah by distorting its nature and best features. Through propaganda, they successfully turned capitalism and individualism into predatory killers and altruism (the real predatory killer) into a benevolent goal that just tried to improve life. As the ideas of Marx, Dewey and other philosophers gained ascendance, those of Locke, the Founders and classical liberals began to fade.

In her excellent book (The Forgotten Man) on the Great Depression, historian Amity Shlaes discusses an important theme that resounded throughout the difficult years of the Great Depression. She reprises a theme put forward by philosopher William Graham Sumner about the forgotten man of the era. She writes:

"About half a century before the Depression, a Yale philosopher named William Graham Sumner penned a lecture against the progressives of his own day and in defense of classical liberalism. The lecture eventually became an essay, titled "The Forgotten Man." Applying his own elegant algebra of politics, Sumner warned that well-intentioned social progressives often coerced unwitting average citizens into funding dubious social projects. Sumner wrote:

'As soon as A observes something which seems to him to be wrong, from which X is suffering, A talks it over with B, and A and B then propose to get a law passed to remedy the evil and help X. Their law always proposes to determine...what A, B, and C shall do for X." But what about C? There was nothing wrong with A and B helping X. What was wrong was the law, and the indenturing of C to the cause. C was the forgotten man, the man who paid, "the man who never is thought of.

"In 1932, a member of Roosevelt's brain trust, Ray Moley, recalled the phrase, although not its provenance. He inserted it into the candidate's first great speech. If elected, Roosevelt promised, he would act in the name of "the forgotten man at the bottom of the economic pyramid." Whereas C had been Sumner's forgotten man, the New Deal made X the forgotten man-the poor man, the old man, labor or any other recipient of government help."[8]

Many think that this focus on the consumer rather than the producer is the very idea that prolonged the depression. I submit that this shift away from the real forgotten man, the enlightened producer, is the very essence of progressivism. As a result of this shift our nation has been poorly served by politicians. In fact, there is a forgotten "ism" that parallels the forgotten man. Where the forgotten man for the progressives was the slave, the hard working American, who silently fed the nation, the forgotten "ism" was the philosophical fountainhead that had to be silenced so that conservatives and progressives could accomplish their

---

[8] The Forgotten Man, Amity Shlaes, Harper Perennial, paperback Page 12

baseless enslavement of the individual. These ideas, reason, the efficacy of the senses, individualism, natural rights and limited government, born in the Enlightenment, had successfully liberated the mind and the body of man so he could flourish and prosper. With progressives and especially with the New Deal, these ideas had to be removed from consideration. That forgotten "ism" is "liberalism", the original philosophy that fostered limited government, liberty and capitalism.

"(In 1936) Roosevelt won because he created a new kind of interest group politics. The idea that Americans might form a political group that demanded something from government was well known and thoroughly reported a century earlier by Alexis de Tocqueville. The idea that such groups might find mainstream parties to support them was not novel either: Republicans including the Harding and Coolidge administrations, had long practiced interest-group politics on behalf of big business. But Roosevelt systematized interest-group politics more generally to include many constituencies—labor, senior citizens, farmers, union workers. The president made groups where only individual citizens or isolated cranks had stood before, ministered to those groups, and was rewarded with votes. It is no coincidence that the first peace-time year in American history in which federal spending outpaced the total spending of the states and towns was that election year of 1936. It can even be argued that one year—1936—created the modern entitlement challenge that so bedevils both parties today.

"Roosevelt's move was so profound that it changed the English language. Before the 1930s, the word "liberal" stood for the individual; afterward, the phrase increasingly stood for groups...."[9]

From the advent of the progressive movement, the political debate in America became hijacked by progressives who began calling themselves "liberals". Not only did they steal the name from an "ism" that was their diametric opposite, an "ism" that saw the individual as sovereign, they even took upon themselves the moral authority to expropriate his property, his mind and his accomplishments. Essentially, they wiped out the only "ism" in our society that defended the individual and they moved the discussion away from protecting the individual to employing coercive measures against him.

The problem for the progressive movement has always been that collectivism and self-sacrifice, do not work. In order to gain the upper hand against capitalism, progressives had to invent atrocities committed by capitalism so they could take over the corporations and blame them for all the failures created by collectivism. It has taken a massive campaign as well as a hugely corrupt re-writing of history to accomplish this most devastating of deceptions.

Yet, even after these decades-long propaganda campaigns and their successes, the Constitution continues to be in

---

[9] Ibid Page 11

the way. Progressives still see our document of freedom as one based on individualism that creates checks and balances to protect people from oppressive government. During these campaigns to undermine the Constitution, the gridlock created by its checks and balances has managed to keep the progressives at bay while individuals continue to prosper. We may be at the end of this process. The progressives are finally winning.

Notice that the progressives have never sought to co-opt the conservative movement. They needed a weak opponent they could blame for supporting capitalism. This strategy was part of their road to victory. Attack a movement that does not want capitalism, accuse it of being in bed with capitalists, and you limit any real opposition. Certainly, they sent a group out called the "neo-conservatives" to pretend to be conservatives while always advancing progressivism, but this has been a dead Trojan horse, so to speak.

In order for their strategy to work, they had to co-opt their only real opposition and turn its arguments inside out. All of the high-minded and evocative terms that animate near universal support for freedom and limited government were turned by progressives in the universities into their destroyers. Masquerading as "liberals", the progressives have gotten away with a lot. For instance they ignored the term "natural rights" and expropriated for their use the income of producers; they ignored the term "individual" and began talking about "victims"; they ignored the term "individual rights" and self-righteously promoted the right to be taken care of (as if they were fighting for a real principle); they changed the term "freedom" to mean freedom from want; they turned our constitutional republic into democracy, the will of the people to coerce the productive; they changed the word capitalists to mean "oligarchs", the very people they enslave and from whom they extort money; they ignored the term "rule of law" so they could make "re-distribution" legal; theft became "social justice"; guaranteed income became "equality"; the pursuit of happiness became part of the corrupt past; and worst of all they collectivized "the environment" and turned it into a term that demanded the destruction of capitalism and industrial civilization.

The progressives' goal was to transition government from one designed to protect the individual to one that would enslave the individual. They wanted to turn man from a self-reliant, self-respecting "man of action" into a self-sacrificing robot devoid of mind and hope for the future – and they want to call it hope for the future.

We can now evaluate and find the true causes of the present condition of the world. Conservatives assigned to reason an inferior position and blocked themselves from arguing for limited government on a solid, believable foundation. What they lost was the strength of conviction that our founders were right. They became defenders of a Pre-Enlightenment past and the status quo; hardly worth listening to by educated people. Today, we are bombarded with arguments that our society was based on religion, that charity was a concept that belongs to conservatives not to progressives, that God and the Ten Commandments were the foundations of liberty and that references to religion and religious morality prove that conservativism is not an advocate of tyranny.

With conservatives unwilling to give up faith in spite of the fact that the Enlightenment had clearly shown reason to be superior in the real world, their goal was to ensure that religion survived the Bill of Rights, that it did not become associated with theocracy and religious persecution. In order to make room for faith, they had to denigrate individualism and reason and exhort man to give up his mind in favor of an ineffable spiritual idea that the Enlightenment had discredited. The result is that individual rights had no defenders and the progressives were given a free ride on the road toward dictatorship. Not only is this state of affairs the fault of progressives, it is even more the fault of conservatives who saw reason as an enemy. The result, the greatest governmental and economic system in the history of mankind had no defenders.

On the other hand, the progressives picked up the banner of reason and gave us pseudo-science to justify their undoing of man's rights and capitalism. This made it possible for them to claim that their un-scientific prejudices, their rationalizations for force and violence were scientific and that their ideas were superior to those of the superstitious conservatives - which gave them an even stronger moral authority. The progressives turned the idea of charity into forced altruism and suggested that society should replace God as the prime mover. Once again, true reason was left out of the discussion.

This left us with only two options, two political "isms" that were both only variants of the very ideas against which the Enlightenment had argued. It was against the basic premises of the conservatives and the progressives that the Enlightenment had made the best arguments; arguments fully defensible and superior; but which had conveniently been pushed out of history with disastrous consequences. Worldwide, the result was poverty, concentration camps, genocide, war, plunder and a constant slide among many nations toward fascism and communism.

We must hold the conservatives and progressives fully responsible for these results. They have been witnesses to the wonders of reason, capitalism and freedom. They have all the evidence they need to make the right choice: classical liberalism; individualism, freedom, capitalism, man's rights, limited government - the philosophy of the Enlightenment. Instead, they chose the lowest values possible: anti-reason and a war against the body and mind of man.

Certainly, there were contradictions among Enlightenment philosophers and these contradictions further weakened the case for individual rights.

Additionally, the Founders also had a difficult task in building a compromise that could consistently argue for freedom, not the least of which was slavery. But the overall thrust of the Enlightenment had proven itself in the decades after the Constitution was framed. Freedom had shown them the light and the way – but few were strong enough intellectually to draw the right conclusions about a proper society. The result is the situation in which man finds himself today; living in the best of all possible worlds and not knowing enough to defend it.

What of the future? How can we defeat the progressives and the conservatives and their totalitarian dreams? I think the best way is to fulfill the promise of the 1st Amendment and develop an opposition that is truly inclusive. We need to reclaim reason and individual rights in our political discourse by rejecting both theocracy and progressivism. We must stand up for the forgotten 'ism'; the true political philosophy of the Enlightenment known as "liberalism".

As John Locke wrote: "...all the power of civil government relates only to men's civil interests, is confined to the care of the things of this world, and hath nothing to do with the world to come."[10]

By following this maxim, we can put those of us who favor liberty on an equal footing against progressives and conservatives. We can re-establish the foundations of our

---

[10] A Letter Concerning Toleration, John Locke

arguments based on reason while we expose the pseudo-science of the progressives; and the potential tyranny of the theocrats; and this will expose their views as truly ignorant and primitive. We can discuss man's rights on a proper metaphysical base that derives from reality rather than another realm of existence. On this foundation, we may yet save our country and create a political majority that could include, not only those who favor religious toleration, but also those who have become disenchanted with the unwarranted force and control being advanced by both the progressives and conservatives. We can see the Republicans for what they are; theocrats who would use force against citizens and who only repeat arguments for liberty when it helps them get votes. We can see the Democrats for what they are; radical descendants of Hitler and Stalin who have learned how to use words to hide from us that they intend to make us slaves.

Hopefully, we will soon be able to say, "Liberalism is dead. Long live liberalism."

Capitalism and Morality

Intellectuals, historians, and economists of free market persuasion have asked themselves, "Why have the historians been predominantly anti-capitalist? Why have they sought to make capitalism appear to be such an evil system when it is responsible for so much good?" Indeed, the history of economic thought is full of intellectuals that have had a selective bias against the achievements of capitalism.

While reading a book on this subject, I noticed that the writers who were trying to defend capitalism offered little argument that completely discredited the profusion of anti-capitalist viewpoints. In fact, there was almost a condescending, apologetic attitude toward men whose words were but crass virulent hatred of capitalism. The book, "Capitalism and the Historians", although excellent in many ways, is weak in one major area: It does not adequately answer the question, "Why do historians distort the facts about capitalism's development?"

None of the distinguished historians whose papers appear in the book attribute to anti-capitalist historians an evil intent. T. S. Ashton refers to "pessimistic views of the effect of industrial change" and says such historians "are not informed by any glimmering of economic sense." Another problem for Ashton is that certain commentators preferred political interpretation of an interventionist nature. He notes also the threading of "facts on a Marxist string." And finally, "The truth is (as Professor Koebner has said) that neither Marx nor Sombart (nor, for that matter, Adam Smith) had any idea of the real nature of what we call the Industrial Revolution. They overstressed the part played by science and had no conception of an economic system that develops spontaneously without the help of either the state or the philosopher. It is, however, the stress on the capitalist spirit that has, I think, done most harm, for, from being a phrase suggesting a mental or emotional attitude, it has become an impersonal, super-human force. It is no longer men and women, exercising free choice, who effect change, but capitalism or the spirit of capitalism. 'Capitalism,' says Schumpeter, 'develops rationality.' 'Capitalism exalts the monetary unit.' 'Capitalism produced the mental attitude of modern science.' 'Modern pacificism, modern international morality, modern feminism, are products of capitalism."

Whatever this is, it is certainly not economic history. It has introduced a new mysticism into the recounting of plain facts. "What should we do with a candidate who purports to explain why the limited-liability company came into being in England in the 1850s with the following words? I quote literally from the scripture: 'Individualism was forced to give way to laissez faire as the development of capitalism found the early emergent stage of entrepreneurial capitalism a hindrance to that rational expansive development which is the very ethos of capitalism.'" Professor Ashton's solution? "But I hold strongly that the future of the subject lies in closer cooperation with the work of economists and that phrases which perhaps served a purpose a generation ago should now be discarded."

L. M. Hacker, in his address, "Anticapitalist Bias of American History," holds that it was not so much Marxist influence that led to the anti-capitalist bias in America, but American political development, primarily, "the recurring struggle between Jeffersonian and Hamiltonian ideas--that is, the creation and maintenance of a weak or a strong central authority; the intrusion of moral questions into the American public debates--slavery, women's rights, prohibition."

This explanation does not answer the question of why the supposed solutions to these matters involved an anti-capitalist bias. Why was capitalism always seen as morally wrong?

Bertrand De Jouvenal, in his "The Treatment of Capitalism by Continental Intellectuals," holds that the Western intelligensia dislike capitalism because of "a grafting of strong feeling onto a weak stem of positive knowledge." He then proceeds to discuss some ways that capitalism is "unpleasant to the intellectuals," and moves to a suggestion that social science may tell us, if it decides to look at such an issue, why the intellectuals act and think as they do. His basic argument is that the peculiar position in society held by the intellectuals could account for an anti-capitalist bias. The "market value of the intellectual's output is far below factor output."

And so it goes. You can read on and on, finding in the defenders of capitalism what appears to be an unwillingness to define the one factor, the one idea that gives rise to the hatred of capitalism. Most of the reasons given in the book are true, in a sense, and to a point, but they do not go far enough. These defenders of capitalism did not sufficiently understand the nature of capitalism and this made it impossible for them to provide for it what its enemies have in profusion: a moral argument.

If one studies the arguments of capitalism's enemies throughout history, one will find, almost to a man, that they hold one philosophical viewpoint, specifically one moral premise: altruism, the idea that it is man's duty to sacrifice for others. They sense, more than do the defenders of capitalism, that a capitalist economic system represents, for most men, an alien code and view of man. Compared to the defenders of capitalism, they know that capitalism is based on selfishness, not charity. They know that if capitalism were to remain pure, their moral code of ritualistic self-sacrifice, as well as their view of man as a helpless pawn under history's or God's or the government's control, would hold no influence over men. If capitalism were allowed to be capitalism, in other words, if the defenders of capitalism were to defend man's right to be moral, to live for his own sake, to be responsible for himself, proudly, passionately, with conviction and pride, the philosophies of Kant, Marx, Hegel and a host of modern offshoots, would be swept away. Men would no longer be intrigued by the ineffable, the vague and undefined, and would instead insist that ideas have real value, real application to their individual lives.

Once Americans begin to stand for their right to be moral; once they begin to fight against the idea that their role in society is to be dutiful sacrificial victims; once they realize that the motive and goal of the detractors of capitalism is nothing more than the destruction of freedom, which means the destruction of their right to live by means of their independent minds; once men begin to demand that government get out of their lives, only then will the progressives become part of the disastrous past that they have created.

The defenders of capitalism do not know that a rational, moral code of ethics is possible. They are, for the most part, altruists themselves (see the conservatives). They adhere to the ideas of altruistic self-sacrifice--so much so that it blinds them to the true nature of capitalism and forces them into the position of being condescending but cheery opponents of men who are neither condescending nor cheery in their hatred of freedom and capitalism.

Altruism is not the moral base of a capitalist system. We can't have a successful capitalist system if we just want to help people. Capitalism requires an independent mind. We must want men to be free to think, we must know living requires work, we must honor the independent mind and we must give credit where credit is due. Altruism requires a mind ruled by the edicts of superiors and it tells man that to be moral he only needs to follow the easiest path of all: the road of sacrifice as virtue. Capitalism requires integrity. Altruism requires that man fight his bodily nature with his spiritual code. Capitalism requires honesty. Altruism requires that one deceive one's own mind. Capitalism requires justice. Altruism requires that justice be suspended among men, that men do society's work by being unjust towards those who refuse to sacrifice. Capitalism requires productiveness. Altruism requires that the productive give away their money. Capitalism requires pride. Altruism requires both humility in some men and pretentiousness in others. Capitalism requires principled action based on abstract concepts tied to reality. Altruism requires Kantian mush, vague, disconnected equivocations, switching contexts, unintelligibility, one reality that is inaccessible by the mind and a second mental universe that is incompetent. Capitalism is a challenge to the individual and it demands his best effort. Altruism demands only envy and hatred of capitalism.

Certainly, the detractors of capitalism have a massive blind spot. Their altruistic premises color their interpretation of historical facts to such a degree that they believe reality conforms to their views. But the defenders of capitalism have a more devastating yet hardly noticed, blind spot. Their evasion of the evil of altruism has kept them from discovering that capitalism is *the* moral system--the system to be advocated with fire and vigor and enthusiasm. It is, after all, freedom among men that makes capitalism successful. It is the possibility of moral living that makes capitalism the moral system.

The idea that liberated our country is that no man should live as a serf. This idea created the most successful nation in the history of the planet. Freedom is what makes America a better place to live. Freedom is what makes Americans the happiest and most tolerant people on this earth. Freedom is what makes us the envy of the world. Freedom is what makes us hated, not because we are decadent, but because, as a nation, we give every citizen the possibility of creating his own happiness by means of his own thought. We are the first nation since the Greeks that made moral living possible on earth.

The mortal enemies of freedom are those who believe that men are moral only when they perform ritual sacrifice. Freedom is the enemy of the man who believes deep down in the core of his being that if men were free, *he* would not be able to survive.

Are most intellectuals and economists biased against capitalism? Yes, as long as they hold that altruistic self-sacrifice is the proper morality for man and for an economic system. Are they right? No, and no amount of condescending argument that says capitalism will achieve the goals of altruists will work against intellectuals who hate themselves and men. No amount of cheery debate against people that want slavery for men will enable capitalism to win. The haters of capitalism must be exposed as haters of men and haters of freedom.

We must fight for capitalism based upon man's right to be

free, his right to property, his right to speak and think and his right to happiness. Consequences, such as the fact that capitalism creates the most vibrant economy, are irrelevant. Capitalism is moral because only free men can be moral.

The Tragic View of Man

I've enjoyed reading the books of Thomas Sowell for many years. I became aware of him in the late 1970s when he burst onto the intellectual scene with amazing analyses of economic trends. His defense of free markets is laudable and he has made many unique and perceptive contributions to our national political debate. Most recently he has written books that have been critical of intellectuals. I just finished one book that brought home to me the problem for conservatives and, especially, why they have found themselves on the losing end of the political debate.

The book, entitled "Intellectuals and Society" is an excellent examination of progressive intellectuals' inability to bridge the gap between their elitist ideas and reality. The first few chapters of the book give an excellent overview of the problems that progressive intellectuals create. According to Professor Sowell, intellectuals are wrong about social solutions because they come at problems from a limited elitist perspective that represents only a small percentage of the total knowledge available in society at large.

I find Doctor Sowell's criticism to be excellent when it comes to analyzing the precarious position of intellectuals who are steeped in specialized knowledge but who have little understanding of the real world. Yet his argument fell apart for me when he compared today's progressives with today's conservatives.

"[Their] vision of society, in which there are many "problems" to be "solved" by applying the ideas of morally anointed intellectual elites is by no means the only vision, however much that vision may be prevalent among today's intellectuals. A conflicting vision has co-existed for centuries—a vision in which the inherent flaws of human beings are the fundamental problem and social contrivances are simply imperfect means of trying to cope with that problem—these imperfections themselves being products of the inherent shortcomings of human beings."[11] (Brackets mine)

Professor Sowell takes for himself the position of the conflicting vision. His preferred vision of man is "...the tragic vision of the human condition that is very different from the vision of the anointed."[12] And, indeed, he joins a long tradition of philosophers and intellectuals who have shared that vision of human beings as inherently flawed. Unfortunately, a fact that he seems to have missed is that this tragic vision of man is also held by the progressives.

I wonder what he would say if I pointed out that the exalted view that intellectuals hold of themselves is not the same view they have of man. Their view of man derives from philosophers such as Kant, Hume and Marx that see men as intellectually incompetent, bereft of the ability to understand reality or the victims of economic factors outside of their control. None of those could be

---

[11] Intellectuals and Society, Thomas Sowell, Basic Books, hardcover page 77
[12] Ibid Page 77

considered an exalted view of man.

You have to ask yourself what is the point of taking the position that man is inherently flawed? Why would conservatives want to start with this premise? And more importantly, why do they think that this position provides a better argument for limited government and capitalism?

As a former Catholic, I am familiar with this view. According to the Church, man is a sinner who would wreak havoc if left to his own "selfish" devices. His only moral constraint is that given to him by God and the church. According to this view, man must follow the Ten Commandments handed down to him by God through Moses. If men do not follow God's Commandments, God will punish them on this earth and after death. Men will only do right because of fear of God's wrath.

Sowell asserts that the vision of contemporary intellectuals (progressives) today is based on an ages old view that sees problems as an outgrowth of social institutions. "In this vision, oppression, poverty, injustice and war are all products of existing institutions— problems whose solutions require changing those institutions, which in turn require changing the ideas behind those institutions."[13] Is Professor Sowell saying that the progressives view is one of hope and that their recommendations are part of some sort of exalted view about actually solving problems? Are we to assume that

---

[13] Ibid Page 76

progressive criticism of institutions such as capitalism and the church are valid? Is he perhaps giving them too much credit? Claiming to have hope for man by forcing them to sacrifice, as the progressives do, is hardly a hopeful concept. Such a hope sounds like a politician's false promise never to come true.

One must wonder if progressives today really threaten to destroy the most advanced, the most just and affluent civilization in the history of the world out of hope for a better future. There is a problem with cause and effect here.

Whether you receive your view of man's nature from Hobbes or Hume, you cannot derive the principles of a free society and the anti-principles of a slave society from the same source; from the view that man is imperfect. The logic of ideas in practice is inexorable; you cannot get around it. If the conservatives and the progressives both have the same basic view of man, the result will be the same social solution...and it is not hope but rubble.

Yet, the question regarding man's nature is the foundation upon which all human action must be based. The answer to that question indicates not only how intellectuals think men will act but how governments will treat them. Does man have rights? Is he to be a slave to the needs of others? These questions are important. The only difference between conservatives and progressives is not that progressives see certain institutions as needing change and that conservatives do not; the vital question is "from where does man derive his mandate for moral action?" Political debates and revolutionary change are not about merely changing institutions; they are about understanding man's nature and dealing with him accordingly.

When Barack Obama says he believes in service to the community, working for and dying for others, the conservatives can only say, 'so do we'. They may counter the progressives with arguments for faith, hope and charity, but the progressives also talk about faith, hope and charity.

The dilemma for the conservatives on this issue is that they've failed to identify the principles that truly reflect what is wrong with the progressive views. They are on the same side as the progressives because they both advocate altruism as their fundamental principle. They have failed to recognize that man's true nature is not that he is imperfect but that he is a creature of reason, a creature perfectly suited for survival and success. The result: the conservatives have nothing to offer against the views of the progressives who also see man as cognitively incapable of understanding reality.

To continue with Doctor Sowell, "In the tragic vision, barbarism is always waiting in the wings and civilization is simply "a thin crust over a volcano." (This quote is from Havelock Ellis. The full statement is "All civilization has from time to time become a thin crust over a volcano of revolution.") The metaphor, "a thin crust over a volcano" used to describe the position of civilization against barbarism is illustrious of the problem that conservatives create for themselves. If civilization is truly a thin crust over a volcano, then what is the point of trying to create a better society? Eventually, the volcano will erupt (into revolution) and destroy that thin layer. If this is our choice, then why should we continue living on that thin crust? (parentheses mine)

Unfortunately, this is the false alternative that conservatives create for themselves. A "thin crust" versus an inevitable explosion is hardly a choice. When they create such false alternatives based on non-essentials, they end up rationalizing false views and eventually taking the side of the progressives. To place one's enemies, the enemies of freedom, in the position of "a volcano", means you know they will win.

Is civilization truly "a thin crust over a volcano"? Or are the principles of a proper society based upon something more fundamental in man's nature that must be recognized and accommodated by government; facts and principles that endure and never explode. Shouldn't we instead strive for a vision of man that will acknowledge his value and thereby help in the creation of a bulwark against the explosion of violence and barbarism? I submit that this bulwark is what the Founders of our nation attempted to create and their vision of man was not at all "tragic".

"In the tragic vision, social contrivances seek to restrict behavior that leads to unhappiness, even though these restrictions themselves cause a certain amount of unhappiness. It is a vision of trade-offs, rather than solutions, and a vision of wisdom distilled from the experiences of the many rather than the brilliance of a few."[14]

This means that civilization is nothing more than "social contrivances" designed to restrict immoral living in order to make a trade-off, to create a balance between immorality (selfishness) and self-sacrifice (the good). What is being traded here is your decision to be productive in return for the government getting a piece of your production. Your punishment for committing the crime of surviving is that you have to pay people who cannot survive. Remember, this is the conservative view. And, to prove it, notice that the desire of President Obama to "re-distribute" wealth is considered by the conservatives to be "the brilliance of a few".

I would like to take issue with the criticism that progressives represent an elite that thinks it is smart enough to make decisions for us. Certainly, they think they are such an elite. But the truth is there is no such elite telling us what to do and how to think. Most of them talk only to themselves. The concept of elitism is a strawman designed to engender hate from the conservative "yokels". Certainly, progressives love when conservatives give them that position of power (and Dr. Sowell certainly does), but the truth is we don't have to listen to them and few of us actually do. Indeed,

---

[14] Ibid Page 78

regardless of what we say about them, they will keep spouting their "superior" knowledge as long as libraries buy their books. That is in the nature of progressivism not elitism.

And to prove that conservatives have no understanding of their own position, Doctor Sowell says, "The conflict between these two visions goes back for centuries. Those with the tragic vision and those with the vision of the anointed do not simply happen to differ on a range of policy issues. They necessarily differ, because they are talking about very different worlds which exist inside their minds. Moreover, they are talking about different creatures who inhabit that world, even though both call these creatures human beings, for the nature of those human beings is also fundamentally different as seen in the two visions."[15]
I'm sure the conservatives appreciate that criticism.

Professor Sowell does not seem to recognize that both philosophical skeptics and conservative philosophers such as Hobbes and Burke saw man in essentially the same way. They both saw man as incapable of understanding reality, in other words, as imperfect. How can the same basic view of man lead to two different solutions in politics? They can't. Progressivism and conservatism are two contrary (rather than contradictory) ideas based on the same premise that will inevitably lead to the same result: enslavement.

---

[15] Ibid Page 78

The reason the conservatives use non-essentials (tragic vision versus anointed vision) in separating conservatives from progressives is that they must evade the hidden motive of the conservative vision. I doubt that Professor Sowell and other conservatives know that their argument on the issue of man's nature is weak and I doubt that they have an ulterior motive. I think they truly want freedom, but even they cannot escape the logical consequences of their arguments. The truth is that their view of man is a false attack and it implies government action against him that would control his individual moral choices. The real goal of religious conservatives, since they became politically prominent, has been to make room for faith in a world that is constantly being transformed by the power of reason. Politically, for the conservatives, that goal can only be accomplished by authoritarian theocracy.

Since religious conservatives want to restrict what they consider to be immoral acts, their advocacy of capitalism necessarily leaves much to be desired. The conflict takes place when you attempt to graft the control of immoral acts (determined by God in the Bible) on a system that is based on the individual's right to decide for himself what is moral action. What the conservative considers to be immoral and selfish may actually be moral and life-serving when viewed from the perspective of the individual and his life (As example, look at past efforts to control sexual activities and attitudes which fall hardest on women and gays).

Economic conservatives therefore must avoid discussions

of morality and stick religiously to economic statistics and the negative consequences of central planning. It also takes some of them to pragmatism, real politick, neo-conservatism and, you guessed it, the inevitability of progressivism (the old "thin crust of the volcano").

In fact, the conservatives have managed to proclaim the superiority of their own stated enemies. "The two visions differ fundamentally, not only in how they see the world but also in how those who believe in these visions see themselves. If you happen to believe in free markets, judicial restraint, traditional values and other features of the tragic vision, then you are just someone who believes in free markets, judicial restraint and traditional values. There is no personal exaltation resulting from those beliefs. But to be for "social justice" and "saving the environment," or to be "anti-war" is more than just a set of beliefs about empirical facts. This vision puts you on a higher moral plane as someone concerned and compassionate, someone who is for peace in the world, a defender of the downtrodden, and someone who wants to preserve the beauty of nature and save the planet from being polluted by others less caring. In short, one vision makes you somebody special and the other vision does not. These visions are not symmetrical."[16] In short, progressives are good and conservatives are evil.

Imagine the following conversation: "Why aren't conservatives good?" asks the conservative.

---

[16] Ibid Page 79-80

"They favor capitalism and self-interest", say the progressives.

"No we don't" say the conservatives. "We want capitalism because we believe that is the best way to achieve "the highest good." We're just like you."

"How is that possible? Isn't capitalism about greedy acquisition and theft from the poor?" ask the progressives.

"Yes, it is," say the conservatives. "But we can control that through regulations and Anti-trust. We just want to manipulate the market so it can achieve 'the highest good.'"

"So do we," say the progressives. "That's why we want to re-distribute wealth."

"But that will create distortions in the marketplace. We don't want any distortions, do we?"

"See," say the progressives. "You really don't mean what you say. You are really just working for those greedy capitalists."

This is called "the moral argument" and it is based on the premise that all human action should be without self-interest; that it should be "for others". The conservatives have no answer except to say they agree; they just want to accomplish social wellbeing in a different way, a way that works. This is not the way to say you stand for the right.

"Trickle down," say the progressives. "Capitalism has failed. We've got a better way. Let's just take the money."

The problem for the conservatives is that pesky little word "self-interest". Because of their altruistic (utilitarian) premises, they just can't get around the idea that capitalism is really about self-interest. They wish it weren't so.

"But the Founders established our traditions and those are good, aren't they?"

The progressives just chuckle at the hypocrisy.

Indeed, self-interest is a pretty bad motivation if you believe that man's duty is to sacrifice for others. The conservatives are stuck with the contradiction. And the dubious utilitarian argument just doesn't seem to work when you've got those left-wing protesters out on the streets in front of television cameras complaining about systemic racism, systemic greed and riches and theft and MONEY, even wild parties and lots of sex too. Once you lay that guilt trip on them, conservatives shut up and vote the way the progressives want.

The progressives have been successful in manipulating the

conservatives into being the agents of "self-interest". Not only have they painted the conservatives into the corner as stealthy advocates of it, but they are also the teachers who have put the proverbial dunce caps on them as well. The conservatives simply cannot get out of that corner until they learn to claim the moral high ground. They are evading the moral arguments for capitalism, the very arguments that hard working Americans would champion and support. These are the arguments that they need if they are to establish the moral fervor necessary to withstand the same progressive arguments that have silenced them for so long - and that make the conservatives into weaklings hardly worth getting out of bed to vote for.

How do they find that moral high ground? You might be surprised to hear that they can't do it by quoting God at every turn. No voter is going to get excited about "moral contrivances" designed to restrict immoral actions. Voters are only going to get excited about the possibility of working hard and keeping their earnings. They need a "selfish" reason to vote not politicians who are afraid to say "capitalism", "individual rights" and "freedom" and "the pursuit of happiness". They need politicians who are going to make the moral case for individual rights and property rights. They don't want moral cowards.

Conservatives have to reject the view that man's nature is part of a "tragic" vision. They must stop focusing their arguments on the idea that man is fallible, that he can only survive by sacrificing for others; they must stop implying that men will always make the wrong moral decisions and that government is there to hold him back. These arguments do not justify freedom; they justify coercion against individuals. Under this view, choosing to live, to create values, to trade values, to organize companies, to be productive, to think, to produce, to make a (huge) profit, to flourish and to enjoy life are all immoral decisions. Why do they agree with that vision of man?

Conservatives must learn to embrace morality by embracing the pursuit of happiness and by being guiltlessly proud of it. It is not a sin to declare that man is a creature with the ability to reason, to choose and to enjoy life.

As I wrote in the chapter, "Capitalism and Morality", "Altruism is not the moral base of a capitalist system. We can't have a successful capitalist system if we just want to help people. Capitalism requires an independent mind. We must want men to be free to think, we must know living requires work, we must honor the independent mind and we must give credit where credit is due. Altruism requires a mind ruled by the edicts of superiors and it tells man that to be moral he only needs to follow the easiest path of all: the road of sacrifice as virtue. Capitalism requires integrity. Altruism requires that man fight his bodily nature with his spiritual code. Capitalism requires honesty. Altruism requires that one deceive one's own mind. Capitalism requires justice. Altruism requires that justice be suspended among men, that men do society's work by being unjust towards those who refuse to sacrifice. Capitalism requires productiveness. Altruism requires that the productive give away their money. Capitalism requires pride. Altruism requires both humility in some men and pretentiousness in others. Capitalism requires principled action based on abstract concepts tied to reality. Altruism requires Kantian mush, vague, disconnected equivocations, switching contexts, unintelligibility, one reality that is inaccessible by the mind and a second mental universe that is incompetent. Capitalism is a challenge to the individual and it demands his best effort. Altruism demands only envy and hatred of capitalism."

The Founders understood that man should be free to make a better life. They knew that he can only do so by identifying reality, understanding what is in his best interest, knowing or discovering how to achieve it and then taking action. They understood that man was good because they, the Founders, had achieved success in life by means of study, practical action and reason. This is the source of our "rugged individualism"; the source of a unique image of a man with the self-confidence and the ability to survive in the wilderness. "Daniel Boone was a man!" This is why they based our society upon the principles of "life, liberty and the pursuit happiness". This is why they limited the power of government to violate those rights.

The Founders understood that freedom makes possible the unhindered pursuit of values. And in order to produce values, a man must have the ability to identify what values are, what human purposes they achieve and not only how to create them but also how to price them, deliver them and discuss their features and benefits for the purchaser. A value can only be created as an outgrowth of a rational process, a thinking process that identifies what is in the maker's and the buyer's self-interest. Capitalism is not about greed but about individual rights and self-interest. This is not the tragic view.

A value must fulfill a proudly selfish need for man because its creation depends upon a person's choice, and in order for you to choose a life-enhancing value, it must first be validated by a process of reason that justifies it in terms of benefit to the valuer. There is no other way to think about values.

Needless to say, conservatives will never argue for capitalism on this basis and this is why you see Professor Sowell attempting to explain the differences between conservatives and progressives on grounds other than an individual's moral right to the pursuit of his own individual happiness.

Contrast the politician of today with an architect such as Frank Lloyd Wright and you will see the difference between a valuer and a nihilist. Wright and his designs are pro-man, pro-life, pro-value. The architect expressed his love of life and of values by means of manipulating natural resources to express in his buildings a concept of priceless utility combined with ultimate beauty and the enjoyment of both. The designs of his buildings expressed so much more than just lines and corners; they expressed the beauty of nature, the organization of natural resources and the feelings of comfort and relaxation. The emphasis on values is so implicit yet so real that you must grow intellectually in order to comprehend the beauty within the mind of the architect. He brings you to a new evaluation of man and all that is possible through him. This is what America and American business is all about, this love of values, this moral high ground, not the sleazy smile of a person who has done nothing notable except write grants for non-profit (and unprofitable) organizations, write books about nothing that he has done and become famous for it. Contrast a Wright with an Obama and you'll see the difference between a person who creates values and one who re-distributes them. One is a businessman who creates life as a natural outgrowth of loving life and the other creates poverty through flim flam and manipulation. One inspires the upward glance; the other inspires the glance of hatred and envy aimed at any man with a mind. And conservatives want to call him an elite with hope for the future.

This refusal by the conservatives to defend capitalism on proper moral grounds has created a situation where there is no opposition to the progressives; and it opens the door to the vilest forms of nihilism. At every turn, President Obama, as President, destroyed values. Whether it was American free enterprise, the sacredness of contract, the rewarding of failure, the bailouts, the dismissing of our allies (and especially of Israel), the hand (full of cash) extended toward dictators, unilateral nuclear disarmament, the unwillingness to take on Iran, socialized medicine, anti-gun policies, Cap and Trade, Union Card Check – everything he did destroyed values.

- The President's antipathy toward free enterprise moved businessmen to hold off investment in the future, froze cash expenditures and destroyed economic recovery.
- His violation of the Chrysler contract with investors established the precedent that destroyed the sacredness and inviolability of contract, a pillar of all great civilizations.
- His boondoggles and "social justice" programs took money from the hands of honest working people, lowered their standards of living and created poverty and hunger.
- His bailouts of banks and other companies turned these companies into oligarchs, harmed their competitors, slowed their growth, caused them to lay off employees and spent inordinate amounts of money in campaign contributions to Democrats.
- His dismissing of our allies on various occasions harmed international cooperation for years into the future and gave dictators a stronger reason to attack our troops, our citizens and our long-time friend Israel, creating a more unsafe world.
- His outreach to dictators and his bowing before potentates sent a clear signal that the United States was under the control of a person who had offered

it up as a sacrificial lamb to be bled by sundry third world non-entities.

- His unilateral canceling of the nuclear defense shield put Poland and other former Soviet satellites inside the gun-sights of Russia and emboldened Iran in her pursuit of nuclear weapons.
- His "ObamaCare" program virtually destroyed the medical profession, reduced the quality of health care, put insurance companies in dire straits and increased costs while also raising taxes and rationing care.

This "victory of nihilism" that Obama has wrought is clearly the fault of conservatives who did not fight for capitalism and freedom in a way that defended the rights of Americans to live, succeed and enjoy life. It has destroyed our ability to produce abundance, but more importantly, it may have destroyed our futures. And because conservatives have too easily attempted bi-partisan cooperation with progressives for so many decades, Americans will think that the conservatives will continue to do what they've always done – promise smaller government but deliver bigger budgets. They will know that the politicians will continue lying to them.

In order to defend limited government, we must defend the capitalist system that is its product. In order to defend the good men who are living moral lives by being productive, we must have a different view of man, a view that sees man (not as a tragic joke who needs to be free because he is stupid), but as a healthy, strong and independent thinker who can make the right decisions about his life and actions – and who needs to be free because it is his right. Only when we defend man's competence, can those who advocate limited government and individual rights capture the moral high ground.

The Founders did not create a society that was based on the imperfectability of man. If any of them expressed that view, they were wrong. In fact, they created a society based on the Enlightenment view of man as a creature of reason and they established the governmental machinery that protected man's mind from the encroachment of unreason. They wanted to foster free expression, free thought, free choices, free markets, in short, liberty; the right of man to live as he chooses without the imposition of government – including without the imposition of a religion.

Jefferson said, "Millions of innocent men, women, and children, since the introduction of Christianity, have been burnt, tortured, fined, imprisoned; yet we have not advanced one inch towards uniformity (of religious thought). What has been the effect of coercion? To make one half the world fools, and the other half hypocrites. To support roguery and error all over the earth. Let us reflect that it is inhabited by a thousand millions of people. That these profess probably a thousand different systems of religion. That ours is but one of that thousand. That if there be but one right, and ours that one, we should wish to see the 999 wandering sects gathered into the fold of truth. But against such a majority we cannot effect this by force. Reason and persuasion are the only practicable instruments. To make way for these, free enquiry must be indulged; and how can we wish others to indulge it while we refuse it ourselves."[17] (Parentheses mine)

Many of the original settlers of our country were concerned about finding a place where they could practice their religion. They were not all concerned about spreading their faith to other men. They had experienced too much of that imposed upon them in Europe. They wanted the freedom to experience and practice their religious principles in their own way. In fact, many of these sects saw religious faith as an individual choice to be contemplated and enjoyed individually in the wondrous and scenic nature that our new land provided. Many of them clearly understood the importance of religious tolerance. We should follow their example.

I think the insecurity of many religious conservatives stems from a feeling that religion will someday go away. I think they are afraid that they don't have an argument against science and reason and they want to convince us that if religion goes away so will freedom. Many of them probably believe this. Their insistence that reason and science (secularism) will turn man into a wild wanton sinful brute is the flaw in their argument. Their belief that man cannot be good without God is intolerant and insulting to many Americans who have fought for religious freedom while also holding to their own philosophies or

---

[17] The Notes on Virginia, Thomas Jefferson

religions. In truth, only free men want to think the highest thoughts; they want to traverse the frontiers of the planet and the universe. If they discover God at the end, it is their right to think as they wish. If they do not, that is their right as well. In truth, only free men can be perfect and that perfection is not a threat to God. Perhaps it is the road to God.

I would like to state that I admire Thomas Sowell tremendously. His defense of capitalism through these many years has undoubtedly required heroic courage and intellectual honesty considering our present political climate. He is truly an admirable man who deserves the highest praise. With that said, I think he is wrong on this crucial issue. If you believe that man is tragically imperfect, the logical conclusion is that you should not leave him free; you should restrict his freedom. And this is clearly what Doctor Sowell advocates when he says that "social contrivances seek to restrict behavior that leads to unhappiness, even though these restrictions themselves cause a certain amount of unhappiness."

In fact, the correct view of man is that he is a creature who should be allowed to discover his moral perfection through his freely chosen thoughts and actions. Because man is perfect in his ability to reason, he must be free. If there is anything in this world to "believe" in, it is the glorious possibilities of man. Only a free man can be moral.

Can Conservatives Save Capitalism?

"In faith and hope the world will disagree, but all mankind's concern is charity." — Alexander Pope

Since I was a small child, I have been struck by the fact that there are many views of the nature of God. What makes one view better than another? How can one individual or religion assume the power to tell the rest of mankind "the truth" about the fundamental questions of the universe – while offering only "belief" as an argument? Is it not better, in the political arena, to remove all of these opinions from the debate and leave men free to decide for themselves by referencing reality? Is this not what our Founders intended when they declared a separation of religion and government while at the same time acknowledging that, statistically, we were a Christian nation?

Radio personality Glenn Beck often mentions Ayn Rand's "Atlas Shrugged" as a major influence on his thinking. He has even said that Ayn Rand changed how he evaluated events in the world. How he reconciles Rand's atheism with his own Christianity is an interesting question. Apparently, like many on the right who have come to admire Rand's ideas, he separates her economic and political influences from her metaphysical and ethical influences. He and many who agree with him prefer to discuss Rand's powerful arguments for capitalism while ignoring her views on religion. When his once frequent guest Yaron Brook, an acolyte of Rand, mentioned his view that man's rights derived from his nature instead of from God, Beck was taken aback and never invited Brook back to his show.

Yet, even Ronald Reagan once said that Ms. Rand's views had influenced him and it seems that this question does not yet bother the right. They still invoke Rand and her writings (Atlas Shrugged in particular) to expose the evil of socialism and government growth. I think that Rand's influence is partly due to the fact that conservatives are desperate to find the best arguments that will stop the tide toward progressive devastation. Rand would say that you can't hold contradictions; your political and ethical views proceed from your metaphysical and epistemological views. Conservatives like Beck and Reagan grounded their political views on religion rather than Rand's "reason" and this resulted in an eclectic mix of religion and free market theory; a fact that left the conservatives lurching with weak, contradictory defenses for capitalism and freedom. Unfortunately, the left will win if the right keeps coming at the issues on anything other than a rock solid foundation. And the issue is too important. If we don't get it right, our children will suffer greatly.

Dr. Leonard Peikoff reminded us in his speech on the New Right, ("Religion versus America") that: "Religion means orienting one's existence around faith, God, and a life of service--and correspondingly downgrading or condemning four key elements: reason, nature, the self, and man. Religion cannot be equated with values or morality or even philosophy as such; it represents a specific approach to philosophic issues, including a specific code of morality."[18]

And if you think I should not use an atheist (Peikoff) to describe religion, I would remind you that Fox News religion contributor (and former priest), Jonathan Morris has written a book to help you, among other things, "(w)ork through the Faith-Hope-Love Cure to rid yourself of self-destructive and self-limiting habits..."[19]

Yet, both Dr. Peikoff and Father Morris have put their fingers on a basic set of ideas that, in a number of forms, you will find everywhere. They both rightly tell us that religion comes down to three basic concepts: faith, God and a life of service or love. Recognize here the connection between Glenn Beck's tripartite philosophy, faith, hope and charity. Faith for Beck starts the thinking process; you have to start with the existence of God. Hope is the result of that belief and a life of service, charity is the moral imperative.

Jonathan Morris	Faith	God	A Life of Service/Love
Glenn Beck	Faith	Hope	Charity

These three condensations of religious fundamentals (faith, hope and charity) are also part of the Reagan

---

[18] Religion versus America, Ford Hall Forum Speech, Dr. Leonard Peikoff, http://www.aynrand.org/site/News2?page=NewsArticle&id=5360&news_iv_ctrl=1225
[19] http://www.amazon.com/God-Wants-You-Happy-Self-Help/dp/0061913561/ref=bxgy_cc_b_img_a

Revolution. You may recall the "swing to the right" that took place during the Presidential campaign of Ronald Reagan during the late 1970s. Many knew that Reagan was seeking the support of evangelicals across the country. They were his base. But many also supported Reagan because of his strong defense of capitalism. He seemed to speak the language of capitalism and he declared free markets to be a major part of his vision for America. Yet, a major influence on Reagan was George Gilder. Who is he?

"George F. Gilder (born November 29, 1939, in New York City) is an American writer, techno-utopian intellectual, Republican Party activist, and co-founder of the Discovery Institute. His 1981 bestseller Wealth and Poverty advanced a practical and moral case for capitalism during the early months of the Reagan Administration."[20]

Gilder's book became a clarion call for a new version of capitalism. Gilder's form of capitalism was not based upon utilitarianism; it was not based on rugged individualism or individual rights. Gilder's capitalism was based on altruism. To quote Gilder:

"One of the chief critiques of capitalism over the years by socialists, liberals, clergymen, and--most notably--the poor has not been of its practical achievements, but rather the perception of its moral character. Most of them have got the idea that the source of wealth comes from

---

[20] http://en.wikipedia.org/wiki/George_Gilder

sinful, anti-Judeo-Christian avarice. Wealth, they often assert, comes from "taking," and therefore the way to combat poverty is to "take" it back and re-distribute it. But as Gilder explains, the *essence* of capitalism is "giving.""[21] (italics mine)

This post, taken from an Amazon.com review of Gilder's book, reveals the essence of Gilder's effort to ground capitalism, not on individual rights, but on religion. Peter Schwartz, in his article ("The New Right") in The Intellectual Activist quotes Mr. Gilder:

"When faith dies, so does enterprise. It is impossible to create through the mechanism of rational self-interest a system of collective regulation and safety that does not finally deaden the moral sources of the willingness to face danger and fight...Without faith and love, self-concern brings an obsession with security, an envy of wealth and an aversion to risk that destroy the gifts of creative capitalism.... Capitalism can be summed up in the language of Scripture: 'Give and you will be given unto, search and you shall find.... Cast your bread upon the waters and it will return to you many fold....' The deepest truth is faith, hope and love.""[22]

---

[21] Amazon.com review by johnthirdearl of George Gilder's Wealth and Poverty: http://www.amazon.com/gp/product/1558152407/ref=s9_simh_gw_p14_d0_i1? pf_rd_m=ATVPDKIKX0DER&pf_rd_s=center-2&pf_rd_r=11FTSJA27TDBG60TPQ5W&pf_rd_t=101&pf_rd_p=470938631&pf_rd_i=507846

[22] "The New Right" by Peter Schwartz, The Intellectual Activist, quoted by Ayn Rand in her Ford Hall Forum speech, The Age of Mediocrity.

Father Morris	Faith	God	A Life of Service/Love
Glenn Beck	Faith	Hope	Charity
George Gilder / Ronald Reagan	Faith	Hope	Love

The truth of the matter is that Gilder wants his capitalism and eat it too. Gilder's ideas took the steam out of the "swing to the right" in the early 1980s. This grounding of capitalism on religion did not catch on. Most advocates of capitalism knew that it could not work and it tempered their enthusiasm for conservative thought. The question: how can capitalism be the moral source for capitalism when it is also the moral source of its opposites; communism, socialism, fascism and welfare-statism?

Even many religious people saw it as a cynical effort to smuggle "ruthless" capitalism into their beloved religious principles which were certainly the opposite of ruthlessness. Yet, Gilder and other "moral majority" Christians continued to be influential and the religious right slowly gained strength until George Bush killed the movement through "compassionate conservativism", another form of the same ideas. Certainly, Beck knows Gilder (because he mentioned him on his radio show) as an important thinker and Gilder has been interviewed on Fox. He is still considered to be a prominent voice for capitalism even today.

What Gilder tried to do for capitalist argumentation is provide an opening to help conservatives become more vocal about defending capitalism. With altruism as a key component of capitalism, they felt it was ok to be proud to be a capitalist. Yet, as with Gilder, who minimized the value of the utilitarian argument for capitalism, you'll find a lot of utilitarianism even today. Check some of his youTube videos to see.

This effort to tie capitalism and altruism into a single argument is pragmatism; a political compromise not only intended for the masses, but also intended for intellectuals who want to use these arguments in conservative universities and publications. It is a "bold leap" that seeks to change society and make capitalism more palatable. Never doubt that conservatives and evangelicals are pragmatists of the worst kind.

Notice, that each of the three principles we are discussing (faith, hope and love) are meant to be loose condensations of more fundamental arguments known in philosophy as Epistemology, Metaphysics and Ethics. Epistemology is the study of how man gains and validates knowledge (in this case, faith); Metaphysics is the study of the nature of reality (in this case, hope); and ethics is the application of these two principles to the realm of human choice and action (in this case, charity). It is only in our age when reason is lacking, when understanding reality is supposed to be impossible, that the same concepts can be expressed so loosely, yet mean the exact same thing when translated into action. Modern philosophy has kept from us the realization that sometimes we are talking about the same ideas, thinking we are deadly enemies, polarizing our debates and refusing to understand each other - when in fact, many of us agree fundamentally. This is true of conservatives and, as we will see, of progressives as well.

Source	Epistemology	Metaphysics	Ethics/Morality
Jonathan Morris	Faith	God	A Life of Service/Love
Glenn Beck	Faith	Hope	Charity
George Gilder/Ronald Reagan	Faith	Hope	Love

It would not be difficult to apply this philosophical foundation to something with which secular progressives might agree. For instance, progressives would never say their philosophy rests on the principles of mysticism, hope and re-distribution. Some progressives would say "reason" rather than "mysticism" but I beg to differ.

Although many secular (progressive) thinkers claim to advocate reason, implicit in their views is an epistemology that essentially relies on a secular form of mysticism. Hegel promoted as "elements of truth" his view that a dialectical process governed both human history and the history of philosophy. This process was based upon a convergence of two principles that he called "thesis" and "anti-thesis" which combined to create a metaphysical synthesis, the next phase of human development. He postulated a sort of cosmic struggle between these two principles but provided no proof for the existence of such a struggle.

Taking his cue from Heraclitus, who postulated that the basic principle of the universe is "change," Hegel concluded that change was foundational in the universe. Yet, even Heraclitus provided no logical foundation for the fundamentality of his premises. So the progressive view is essentially a form of accepting a principle of fundamental motion in the universe without proof – taking the explanation itself as its proof. This is a contradiction, a secular form of faith in the name of science.

Of Hegel's marriage of philosophy with history, Windelband wrote: "The fundamental thought, right in itself, thus led to the mistake of a construction of the history of philosophy under the control of (Hegel's) philosophical system."[23] (Parentheses mine) The result was a history of thought dependent upon Hegel's singular interpretations and nothing more – his faith. Hegel's god was the "Absolute".

Upon Hegel's foundation, a more virulent form of mysticism was developed by Karl Marx. Marx's mysticism was derived in the same way as Hegel's. He merely changed the definitions of the cosmic struggle and postulated economic systems as fundamental to the universe (again without proof or validation). It consisted of positing the economic class struggle as the fundamental principle that moved thesis and anti-thesis toward synthesis. For Marx, the historical process was a struggle between economic systems (or classes) where

[23] A History of Philosophy" by Wilhelm Windelband, Googlebooks version.

the thesis, the existing system at any particular point in time, was opposed by its anti-thesis, the next stage of history. Marx held that the thesis, capitalism, was being opposed by its anti-thesis socialism. According to this view, the class struggle was inexorable; the process was a fixed system, as certain as a scientific fact that no man could change. Capitalism was doomed scientifically by this historical materialism and would be defeated by socialism. It was merely a matter of time.

By making capitalism the inevitable loser of this imaginary historical struggle, Marx succeeded in justifying for communists, fascists and progressives any act of violence, hatred, prejudice and legal plunder against capitalism and capitalists. If you did not adhere to the inevitable coming of socialism, which was nothing more than sacrifice of the rich to the poor (the same altruism countenanced by religion), then you were old-fashioned, out-of-date, reactionary and evil – and should be killed. And because socialism was "just," Marx countenanced violent revolution in order to hasten the inexorable movement of history. In other words, he countenanced haste, the manipulation of history, because, after all, socialism was the next phase of history (and it was good).

Though Marx claimed to be a champion of science and atheism, a more sinister form of mysticism than Marxism has not been attempted. Like Hegel, Marx and the Marxist revolutionaries merely "believed" in the inevitability of socialism. Today, the "certainty" and moral fervor of progressives and other revolutionaries against capitalism is founded on this secular form of "faith."

In many respects, Marxists and their philosophical apologists created a cottage industry that helped them dominate the universities while incorrectly interpreting everything from history to psychology to anthropology and even modern societies according to the fictional class struggle. All they had to do was talk about the class struggle and (supposedly) this made them intelligent and scientific.

Upon the basis of this mysterious class struggle some of the most atrocious lies could be spouted and given the imprimatur of "science." The result was the death of millions of "spies" and "enemies of the people" who were guilty of merely wanting to live productive lives.

The Marxist assumption that this "dialectical" struggle will result in the eventual victory of socialism is one of the biggest scams of modern philosophy and economics. There simply is no proof that this struggle exists. It amounts to a bluff, a con man's effort to wish a false idea into existence; to create a self-fulfilling prophecy through pseudo-scientific mystical incantation. Anyone who accepted Marxist views of history merely accepted them on faith because the "sounded" right. One cannot prove the future.

Today, progressives consider themselves to be more educated than conservatives because Marx said that his intellectual constructs were science. This added power to his ideas and encouraged more people to accept them. Yet, there is no science in Marxism; only pseudo-science; and this false idea led a whole continent to take a bold and deadly leap into socialism. If this isn't ignorance, it is ignorance squared. It is pragmatism.

Upon this foundation, Marx postulated socialism as the only hope for mankind. His re-distributionist foundation was supposed to provide for man a shining, prosperous and happy future. All that men have to do is sacrifice *now* so their children will experience that shining future. Once again, we end with the ethics and the politics of altruism, the same place where Glenn Beck, George Gilder, and Ronald Reagan wind up.

Source	Epistemology	Metaphysics	Ethics/Morality
Father Morris	Faith	God	A Life of Service/Love
Glenn Beck	Faith	Hope	Charity
George Gilder/Ronald Reagan	Faith	Hope	Love
Georg Hegel	Dialectic	History	Sacrifice
Karl Marx	Historical Materialism	Prosperity	Socialism / Communism / Altruism

Yet, we need not go all the way to Hegel or Marx to identify what a modern progressive, eager for power might say. How about President Obama? He has made every effort to express his deep religious principles and although he holds the Marxist critique of capitalism, his view of collective salvation and his re-distributionist philosophy essentially matches that of the entire group under discussion.

Source	Epistemology	Metaphysics	Ethics/Morality
Father Morris	Faith	God	A Life of Service/Love
Glenn Beck	Faith	Hope	Charity
George Gilder/Ronald Reagan	Faith	Hope	Love
Georg Hegel	Dialectic	History	Sacrifice
Karl Marx	Historical Materialism	Prosperity	Socialism / Communism
Barack Obama	Faith	Hope	Charity/Sacrifice

You may be surprised to see that the ideas of progressives and conservatives, in terms of fundamentals, are as closely related in the chart above. The reason for this is that Kant, one of the most dominant thinkers of our modern age, admitted that he had developed his philosophy in order to protect religion from the Enlightenment (from reason). This means that one of the people who is intellectually responsible for Marxism and progressivism, was also a deeply religious person who wanted to keep, as the field of philosophy moved into secularism, all the premises of religion.

Regarding hope, this concept is used by all of these thinkers as a metaphysical principle. They are obligated to do so because their goals of enslaving men would not be possible without deceiving men about their true goals. It is part of the pragmatist mindset. For religion, God, residing in heaven, was manifest to man as hope of salvation in heaven by practicing virtue on earth. Some Christians extend that hope into the real world in order to expand the scope and power of the God principle--God's intervention into the affairs of men means that God "governs" men – the kind of government that our Founders warned about.

If you really advocate capitalism, you must first develop the correct fundamentals that support capitalism logically, the right philosophy. These are reason, political freedom and the pursuit of happiness. This is implicitly what the Founders of our country advocated. This also was explicitly argued for by Ayn Rand in her writings.

One key difference between all the views we have discussed above and those of Radical Capitalists is that religious views fundamentally oppose the pursuit of happiness and self-interest. This is because they are animated by altruism which requires that man give up his mind to faith, that he is owned by the collective and that his only proper moral action is to sacrifice for others. The advocacy of altruism (by men such as Beck and religious conservatives as well as progressives) actually destroys hope and reason as it is an outgrowth of unreason and faith. It leads eventually to nihilism and dictatorship. For details on the causes of nihilism and dictatorship, I refer you to Ayn Rand's writings.

Source	Epistemology	Metaphysics	Ethics/Morality
Father Morris	Faith	God	A Life of Service/Love
Glenn Beck	Faith	Hope	Charity
George Gilder / Ronald Reagan	Faith	Hope	Love
Georg Hegel	Dialectic	History	Sacrifice
Karl Marx	Historical Materialism	Prosperity	Socialism / Communism
Barack Obama	Faith	Hope	Charity/Sacrifice
Radical for Capitalism / Founding Fathers / Objectivism	Reason	Political Freedom / Rational Egoism / Hope	The Pursuit of Happiness

You will notice that each of these three principles of Ayn Rand is the opposite of those provided by our religious leaders and progressives. Reason holds that reality is accessible to the senses; it accepts nothing on faith and looks for answers in the real world. Reason also implies political freedom and self-determination which yields hope for the future, not in the religious sense, but in the metaphysical sense; that man must choose to think if he is to have a life worth living on earth; it is his choice – and, rather than asking him to sacrifice for others, his morality must be based on his rational self-interest, on the pursuit of happiness and not upon altruistic self-sacrifice. That's the difference between George Gilder and Ayn Rand.

These principles of Ayn Rand, I submit, are the foundation for capitalism; they make it possible for us to actually argue for the right type of society – with vigor, certainty and moral certitude.

Reason is the faculty that seeks to answer man's most fundamental questions regarding the nature of existence (metaphysics), how man should use his mind (epistemology) and what he should pursue in life (ethics) as well as what kind of society will best enable him to live successfully on earth (politics).

A knowledge of reality is the base upon which man lives. Reason, not a supernatural being, must be the metaphysical base from which he makes judgements about what is proper (good). In fact, life is the only standard for proper action. The good, in essence, is man-made.

Reality is what it is and it is possible to flourish and thrive on earth if we use reason to understand nature. Nature gives us the possibility of happiness but it does not give us happiness. Happiness can only come from choice, reason, a moral code and a way of seeing the world that yields understanding and knowledge. In other words, reason makes possible egoism which makes hope for the future and rational egoism possible.

Free will is not about mindless choice but about the capacity of man to focus his attention, to use reason, or not. The idea of faith then relegates choice solely to the question of rationalistic deduction from the existence of God, a point that is philosophically debatable at best and has so many variations that it is impossible for man to unify around any singular principle. That's why you can develop the very same principles from the concept of God for conservaties and the "Absolute" for Marxists and progressives. Both concepts (accepted on faith) remove man from thinking about the daily and long-term choices he must make. Only reason can help him accomplish his basic emotional, material and value needs. Faith in God makes sacrifice into man's only real choice; a choice demanded by God – which is really not a choice. The Absolute, for the very same reason, leads to the very same derivative concepts (false hope and destructive charity). This is not the stuff upon which to base a social order or a "social contract."

If we are going to be successful in winning back our free society, we must stand for ideas that can be defended on this earth, ideas that can help us drive home the message: "I want to be free" with an unrelenting force of argument. We need to stand, again and again, for individual rights, property rights, the freedom of choice and limited government. We need to be moral agents for freedom, true radicals for capitalism standing firm upon what we know, standing firm on arguments that could change the minds of people who are not swayed by conservative ideas such as faith, hope and charity. We need to insist on our rights, especially among those who are not swayed by conservative ideas.

Let's move the discussion forward in time.

"Liberty University is a place where they really have true champions and you have a simple creed that you live by, to be, really, champions for Christ. Whether you're called to be a missionary overseas, to shepherd a church or to be a leader in your community, you are a living witness of the gospel message, of faith, hope and love. And I must tell you, I am so proud as your president to have helped you along over the past short period of time." – President Donald J. Trump

Donald J. Trump	Faith	Hope	Love

Can conservatives save capitalism? The answer is "No." Men cannot save capitalism without standing up for individual rights. They must proudly declare man's right to be affluent, his right to capital accumulation, his right to earn massive amounts of money (if he chooses to be highly productive), and his right to pursue happiness in any way that his rational mind decides.

We cannot save capitalism without also recognizing the role of reason in man's life and in his ethics. We cannot save capitalism by declaring that we really seek the same goals as the collectivists (charity) and that we merely take issue with the means of reaching that goal. We will lose that argument every time.

Compassionate conservativism is not something people can cheer about. Not only does it not appeal to those who want a rational foundation for capitalism, it cannot change the minds of honest people who have mistakenly accepted on faith a progressive's view of history.

One does not have to dive into the depths of the ineffable in order to provide a foundation for principles that are effable. Man is here, on earth, he lives on earth, thinks on earth, his nature functions on earth and his mind is fully capable of understanding, learning and thriving...on earth. If you want to understand how to support arguments for capitalism, look at the facts.

You must ask yourself, with the basic premises of the right and the left today, who would support dismantling the welfare state? Neither the progressives nor the conservatives can do it. Who would have the courage to say that we aren't going to take care of people (who really don't need to be taken care of)? Who would not slump into nothingness under an onslaught of leftist rhetoric that blames the right for hating the poor, wanting to kill the poor, wanting to destroy our (socialist) values and being in the pay of capitalists? Certainly not the conservatives.

The conservative could only say that he too wants to help the poor, but he would prefer that such help be offered voluntarily. The left and the right would laugh and call him a defender of the rich. And, the left, with full righteousness and conviction, would scream that you can't help the "helpless" when everyone is out for themselves and stealing from the poor. As long as altruism is considered the "practical" way to run society, you'll never be able to make a change that will "work."

If you want to know why there is so much violence coming from the left from such groups as Antifas, this is the reason. These groups falsely take the moral upperhand and assume they have a right to force a socialist history into existence.

Final note: I would like to state explicitly that I am not a spokesperson for the philosophy and ideas of Objectivism and Ayn Rand. My understanding of her philosophy is strictly my own.

The Tea Party Protesters – the Left's New Inferior "Race"

Why did the Left hate Tea Party protesters when they came onto the scene in response to President Obama's election? Why did the left call these protesters fascists, racists, violent people and tea baggers (a sexual slur)? How is it they were able to get away with these spurious insults when, in another time and place, they would be the first to protest such insults made by others towards them? I think it is very simple. The Left displayed the same thought process against Tea Partiers that racists used against other groups in the past.

Racism is the idea that individuals with certain physical characteristics also contain "racial characteristics" such as ignorance, stupidity or inferiority. It is the practice of assigning negative "markers" to groups of people seen as threats or otherwise hated.

To the leftists, Tea Party people and other pro-capitalist voters were the new inferior "breed", the people who deserved ridicule and exclusion from society because they were a threat to the "Master" establishment. The collective markers the left singled out were the characteristics that the leftists invented in order to insult them; such characteristics as uneducated, unwashed, Astroturf, racists, fascists, bigots, etc. Indeed, the left's discrimination toward Tea Party protesters had the same motive, the same method, the same hatred, the same unfairness, the same collectivism, the same insults and the same results, which are isolation, unpopularity and exclusion: in a word, it is the same thought process as racial discrimination.

What is the connection between racist Dixiecrats and today's left? Both groups think in terms of collectives, not individuals. The only difference between the two is that the hated collective for the left, the new hated "race" is made up of individuals who advocated individual rights, whereas, for the Dixiecrats, the hated group included blacks who had been given their individual rights. In both cases, the excluded characteristics is that today's Democrats and yesterday's Dixiecrats both opposed individual rights for American citizens.

In ridiculing the Tea Party Movement, the left sought a scapegoat to blame for its own mistakes. Leftists today lead a very precarious existence for several reasons. Their government solutions do not work. The jobs bill has failed, the American people do not support the Health Care bill, and their poll numbers kept going down...but worst of all: the Tea Party people kept raising issues for which the left had no answers.

Tea Partiers were among the first people who declared that the left does not deserve the moral upper hand it assumed for itself. The Tea Partiers said that the left's coercive activities violated the Constitution. Such criticisms were alien to the left's thought process and, frankly, they didn't expect to be opposed on such grounds. So they call such arguments reactionary, fascist and right wing.

But that didn't help their insecurity. The Tea Party people insisted that it was the progressives who caused the financial collapse, not capitalism. They said that socialism had failed due to the Community Reinvestment Act (that caused faulty loans to be approved) and the Federal Reserve (that caused the housing bubble). In fact, the Tea Party people insist that the sub-prime financial debacle was a direct result of the left's re-distribution schemes not of a free market.

But there is a more important issue that encouraged massive discrimination against people in the Tea Party Movement. It was not only that Tea Party people stood opposed to the loss of their individual rights, certainly this was true, but a far bigger reason was the tremendous amount of power and money that the progressives and their oligarch friends stood to lose if they were to be defeated politically. Though they knew they would rule over a diminished economy, it was still a huge economy made up of some of the most talented and productive people in the world – and what was most disheartening for the left was that those very productive people were, in large measure, in the Tea Party.

Think about how this opposition to the progressives complicated their new form of "political" profiling (as opposed to racial profiling) and how they defined the enemies of society; the left had expected "the people" to rise up with them against the capitalists. They had not expected "the people" to rise up against the left. Indeed, the left has spent decades of taxpayer money concocting huge problems such as CO2 emissions, insurance company profits and financial "greed" in order to 'sell' their re-distribution scams. Not only have they invested huge sums of their own money (that they made from selling short in the stock market) but they've also invested stolen money from government grants and other boondoggles, and, after all of that investment, they may not be able to enrich themselves after all. Can you feel the anger building?

If anything will generate hate among looters and plunderers it is the tremendous problem created when the very people they want to loot do not buy into the "sacrifice" scam. This means huge losses to the leftists. Do you wonder why they passed their legislation in spite of the opposition of the American people? Do you wonder why they verbally attacked the Tea Parties? They must engage in massive amounts of vitriol and hatred because there is too much on the line...so much that, well, there are going to be some very unhappy "investors" if the leftist schemes fail - people who don't like to be disappointed, if you know what I mean.

So, like the Dixiecrats of the old south who once hated and ridiculed Blacks, the left had to accuse the Tea Partiers of corrupting social cohesion, because for them it was true, the society they needed, a society ripe for exploitation, may not actually be so ripe. Those pesky Tea Party people stood up against their plundering of the American economy.

So now you understand why, today, the left doesn't argue on issues but instead attacks the opposition with meaningless and pointless insults. That's all they know because they've lost the mantle of morality long ago. Their highest level of morality is plotted across a negative scale consisting of a community organizer who teaches them to use ridicule against their enemies and who believes that the end (theft) justifies the means (corruption); and a politician who schemes against productive businesses for a campaign contribution (from corporations); or of a union organizer whose thuggish tactics force people to join unions so he can continue to plunder his depleted pension plan; or of a hedge fund manager who organizes a timely flight from the stock market in order to steal the savings of American 401Ks.

I'm certain I will be accused of gross unfairness in criticizing the corruption of the left while ignoring the "good things" they are trying to do. Some of this criticism will come from the "moderates" of today who think Obama is nothing more than a good guy trying to do the right thing. I think these people have their heads in the sand and, for that very reason, they are the most intolerant when it comes to opposition against the left. These are the "fair minded" people who are "too busy" to pay attention to what is happening in our country and don't know the difference between a Karl Marx and a Thomas Jefferson (and they don't want to know), or a Van Jones and a Yaron Brook; they see the issue as an argument between extreme personalities and nothing more. They think freedom-loving Americans are too concerned about what Rush Limbaugh says or they think that Americans spend too much time watching Fox News. For these people the problems in our nation are caused by people who just "hate" the President (Obama), not because he was a radical bent on total domination of *their* lives but because he was a Democrat (or black). They are missing the point.

They can't conceive of the idea that some Americans opposed the President, not out of hate, but because they understand that re-distribution does not work and never has worked. In fact, the *true* "moderate" was the person who stood against everything Obama did. This is because everything he did was re-distribution and it was his policies that were at the extreme. There was no malice in recognizing that, and no radicalism, except in the sense that radical thinking is thinking in terms of fundamentals.

I've written before about the fact that the people to whom money is re-distributed by government never spend that money as sensibly as the person who first earns it. And quite often, the earners save that money to invest it in businesses that create jobs while government recipients merely spend it on consumption. The same principle applies to the oligarchs who steal the taxpayer's money through various government/business alliances fostered by corrupt politicians. That money, obtained by corrupt means, will most often be invested in poorly managed factories, hiring unconcerned employees and producing poor quality products no one wants.

So when someone thinks that the progressives are merely trying to make things better, they betray the fact that they are unable to recognize the fallacies inherent in their own re-distribution schemes.

A good example would be someone who says he has a solution to the financial crisis. We should make banks pay some of their profits into a re-distribution program that gives loans to poor people so they can buy homes. This would help people and improve the economy says the advocate of this scheme. Yet, he ignores the fact that a similar program (the CRA) caused the financial meltdown in the first place and by doing exactly the same thing that the new program will do.

The idea of taking money from the owners of productive companies is a violation of their rights and it gives money to people who feel entitled to it but don't have the pride of having earned it. This is the immorality that Obama supporters completely overlook and this is what the Tea Party people opposed. Who would have thought?

Progressives have only one solution to our nation's problems: make productive people pay so others may benefit...and this is the very sort of "solution" that never works - and it causes our nation's problems. It is this sort of solution, and many more like it, proposed by the left (financial regulation, Cap and Trade, Health Care, and more) that are bringing about the biggest looting spree in the history of our country.

The real solution offered by the Tea Parties was to stop all of this foolish spending and let the people solve the nation's problems through trade and good business practices. So who's the radical? Who's looking out for the nation? They are the advocates of individual rights whose opinions the left wants to silence and ignore.

The Tea Party protesters were discriminated against unfairly because they were standing on the ramparts to fight for their freedom. These courageous people were the left's new "inferior race" that refused to be shoved to the back of the bus by hateful verbal thugs. Certainly, they were a threat to the progressive schemes of plunder; but they were also a threat to the Republican schemes of plunder; a threat to the Karl Roves of the world.

What the progressives have failed to understand is that in a free society, every person is an individual and he cannot be looted if he and many others stand up for individual rights. What the left and mainstream conservatives fail to understand is that an educated citizenry is the last stand against thievery and plunder; the advocates of individual rights are the last hope for civilization. They are the genesis of a coming movement called the Radicals for Capitalism of which I am a member.

Is Fox News Fair and Balanced?

I remember when the only television news stations in Indianapolis were CBS, ABC and NBC. There was little questioning of the news that their pioneering talking heads gave; but I remember also some frustration from conservatives that their viewpoints were not being represented. What's new?

My family was made up of Kennedy Democrats and we didn't really want to hear what the Republicans were saying (Before Kennedy, we did like Eisenhower as President but remember more his golf playing than any opinion he espoused). Those were times of economic growth and as long as Eisenhower was playing golf, we knew he was not doing any harm.

I admired Kennedy for his youth and strength. He seemed to be a man of action and he inspired me to pay attention to what was going on in the world. He elevated politics in this country, at least in my lifetime; but now, I don't think that was a good thing. Because of Kennedy, politics became a sport that everybody watched.

I'd prefer a politics to which we don't have to pay attention on a regular basis; a politics that leaves the people alone and doesn't have to be constantly fixing crises; a politics that supports society by making sure it is free rather than constantly seeking to expand its own power over people. It is possible to have a politics over which people don't have to constantly worry. If people aren't constantly wondering what government will do to them next, they can live much happier lives.

I think that is the way it was intended to be. I think our founders established the rights of man, individual rights, in order to keep government from constantly meddling in our lives. In fact, for many decades we did not even have a national income tax. Once we did, politicians began spending their time vying for power so they could control the money pit and turn its benefits toward themselves and their friends. It is not about doing good for the people, it is about the cynical use of "good intentions" to launder money.

The public today clamors for honesty and freedom while the demagogues clamor for more power. They lie to us that they are really on our sides, we vote for them, then all the promises dissolve...on to the next election. I find it ironic that during the last election Congress' approval ratings were in the low double digits while 95% of them were re-elected. Something is wrong and it appears that those who have power have learned how to keep it in spite of low popularity, huge and embarrassing scandals and outright corruption. The scam is pretty simple; smile a lot, lie a lot, ask people to trust you and brag about how much of the taxpayers' money you brought back to your district. Get people to say, "I like that guy; he's a straight shooter," and you can get elected time after time. It doesn't hurt to also get control of the election machinery. The result: the most corrupt of our politicians, those caught in heinous acts of theft and fraud, are the ones re-elected with the highest margins of victory.

The media is part of the problem. The role of the media should be to present the facts of any story without ideological or political distortion. It should also select for publication stories that expose corruption and graft. Instead it selects stories that only make one party look bad while the other party engages in massive fraud and money laundering.

There is a clear bias in the mainstream media and they are losing viewership due to it. It is not that the public has swung to the right. It is that the public is more educated and demanding more balanced reporting. People can tell a slanted story when they see one. Hence the welcomed ascendance of Fox News, a network dedicated toward a more open and fair presentation of both liberal and conservative views. Fox has leveled the platform politically and given voice to many people shut out of the mainstream media. But all networks should be "fair and balanced". Shouldn't they all present news without bias? Why should there even be such a question as which network is fair and balanced?

Yet, I question whether Fox News is really fair and balanced. Are they doing us a great favor by presenting all sides of an argument? More to the point, are the leftists and the rightists really opposites?

I remember from my Introduction to Logic course that arguments fall into two categories: (1) arguments between contradictories and (2) arguments between contraries. A contradictory represents two opposite points of view. Using the principle of "excluded middle" you are either for a given point or you are against it. The key in such argumentation is for the news network to make sure the two opposing views are true contradictories, that is, fundamental divisions rather than just two opposing views among many views. In argument, and in reality, two contradictory propositions cannot both be true.

Yet, with contraries, two propositions can both be false. An argument between two contraries is based, not on opposite principles, but on disagreements over like principles. A contrary might include a liberal and a conservative view on forced charity or welfare. Both parties favor it so there is no real disagreement except how to do it. This is not a fundamental argument. The real fundamental is whether to do it or not. An argument among contraries on any issue does no service to the truth since it leaves the door open to polarization over non-essentials and assumes that all people agree on the fundamental. On this question Fox News may as well be CBS or MSNBC. Ouch!

For instance, society is not improved when we argue for a point that enables politicians to re-distribute without question. On this issue and many others, the question should not be how much or how fast we should move to solve a particular "problem" but whether the government should re-distribute wealth at all. This applies to every major government boondoggle; especially government bailouts, government forced bankruptcies, stimulus bills and socialized medicine to name a few.

I submit that most Fox News reporting, though a welcomed departure from propaganda media, is still not fair and balanced because it assumes, most often, that we all favor a mixed economy; an economy in which there is a great deal of government force and some political freedom. The Fox News talking heads are arguing about contraries, not contradictories.

Additionally, a great deal of Fox reporting is religious in nature. I assume the premise for presenting these stories is to give religion a voice that it doesn't have on other networks. This is fine but many viewers would prefer straight news not religion. Religion should be sought out rather than forced upon all viewers. This is why I never watch Fox and Friends in the morning. Too many appeals for charity. Where's the news? Mixed in.

For instance, what does it mean to be left or right? Do you know that these divisions were invented in Germany during a time when statism was in full swing, where the only real opposition was among two views of statism? These divisions, left vs. right, were among two contraries, not two contradictories. Commenting on the divisions in pre-Nazi Germany, Ludwig von Mises said the following:

"The mere fact that these two groups (left versus right) are fighting each other does not necessarily prove that they differ in their philosophies and first principles. There have always been wars between people who adhered to the same creeds and philosophies. The parties of the Left and of the Right are in conflict because they both aim at supreme power."[24]

One thing that can be said of the left (communists) and the right (fascists) in Germany was that at least they both called their systems socialism. Yet, they agreed on one fundamental issue: the government has the right to impose its will on the people...whether they like it or not. "Left versus Right" in Germany was a division among fellow-travelers...not fundamental enemies. These parties were allies vying against each other for power with the basic question of whether the government should engage in coercion already settled.

In our country, since the advent of the progressive movement, the left has led the country further and deeper into fascism while the right has merely argued about how far and how fast we should go. When Fox News presents two "opposing" views on many political topics it is not really presenting opposing views; it is presenting two parties with essentially the same fundamental views. How can we make a real choice when the only choices presented on the news are among parties with the same opinion; that opinion being that the government should grow? How can we make real change, let alone have a real debate, when the debate is rigged?

---

[24] Ludwig von Mises, Omnipotent Government, Libertarian Press, Paperback P 177

The proper division of opinions, the two contradictories today, are statism versus limited government; not Democrat versus Republican, not progressive versus conservative, not left versus right. Yet, nowhere does Fox News attempt to be truly fair and balanced in politics. There are still many viable positions that are locked out of the debate, even on Fox News, and this is a disservice. Where are the advocates of a truly limited constitutional government on Fox News? They are barely heard. If they do promote such people, it is not in debate but in individual interviews. We should see more of these people taking on both Republicans and Democrats. Then, perhaps, we can get back to a society where we don't have to worry what government is going to do to us.

Do Americans Know their Rights?

The history of our nation is a struggle between two opposing views of man's nature. These views have been offered to man during two distinct periods of our history. The first period, that of our nation's founding, and for about 140 years afterwards, was the period of the Enlightenment's view of man. I'll let William Peters' description of our founding fathers summarize:

"Basic to their (the founders) shared assumptions was a belief that just as there were laws that governed the physical world, there were natural laws that governed society, laws that could be understood through reason and experience and which men ignored at their peril. The purpose of civil government, as the seventeenth-century English philosopher John Locke had explained was to enforce these natural laws, the most important of which was that no man should take from another his natural rights to life, liberty, and property. A government that failed to protect these rights had lost its reason for being and deserved to be changed or overthrown by the people it governed."[25]

This view reflected what I call a positive theory of man's value. It assumed that man was good, that he could make his world better through the use of his mind. The concept of "rights" was an acknowledgement that, when man was left alone, that is, when his peaceful activities were protected by government, he was free to flourish. These

---

[25] William Peters, A More Perfect Union, Crown, Page 35

rights were a result of real-life discoveries; the founders had learned through experience that man survived by the use of his mind, and they induced a new principle; that man was endowed with rights by his nature and by the nature of existence. This was the lesson of the Enlightenment and the inhabitants of the New World had definitively verified that lesson through their own living. They had learned that free living meant good living. And it gave them a brilliant new insight: Freedom from tyranny was a requirement of survival; they had learned about the power and import of the universal rights of man; they invented a new type of society, a new idea, a better idea...truly this was change. They were convinced that "Man's mind is opened, or opening, to the rights of man."[26]

The founders were well aware of the hardships they had borne under a different system, a tyranny represented by a monarchical form of government which required acquiescence to the will of a despot; a system that made the individual a servant to the King and/or to a religious viewpoint, neither of which allowed dissent and self-determination, both of which required that man sacrifice his mind and his production without question. The Boston Tea Party was one the first demonstrations of the intellectual revolution that would overturn this tyranny.

The other opposing view of man came with the advent of progressivism during the age of collectivism. This view

---

[26] (2) Thomas Jefferson - private letter

holds that man cannot be moral unless there is an enlightened authority directing his actions. A basic premise of the progressives is that production is theft; that when a man uses capital to make something in a Laissez Faire society, he is taking it from the poor. It held that civil society should force the capitalist and the individual to sacrifice his production and property for the sake of the state which was the representative of the collective. The progressive movement evolved, during its history, from a movement promising economic plenty through labor agitation and central planning (the dictatorship of the proletariat) and, after failing to produce economic success, to one that operated beneath the structure of a capitalist society "agitating" for re-distribution under various disguises such as fairness, equality and utopia.

The century dominated by the progressives included some of the most vicious wars in the history of mankind (the 20th century) while the century dominated by the Founding Fathers was one of the most peaceful and prosperous (19th century). The Founders' theory of man left men free and produced one of the most dynamic societies in history while the progressives agitated and fought one another for economic control of capitalism creating a society characterized by constant war, racism, genocide, concentration camps; eventually culminating in the utter decimation of both Europe and Japan. The key premise of the progressives has always been the same, regardless of the system they espoused. That premise was held by the Weimar Republic, Nazi Germany, Fascist Italy,

Socialist England, Soviet Russia, Communist China, Roosevelt's New Deal and today's Welfare Statists in the USA (liberals and conservatives). Simply put it is the idea that the government owns all individuals and must force them to sacrifice for the collective.

If you think that the Obama administration has nothing in common with the dictatorships of the last century, you haven't been listening to their statements. They hold that the government should solve all problems and that the government need not consider the Constitution as an impediment to reaching their goals. Today's progressives say they only want to make capitalism better (which they cannot do), and they insist they are not connected to the ideas and philosophies that brought so much destruction and bloodshed. The truth is that they are direct descendants of the views held by both the communists and fascists who fought each other in the streets for control of Europe. Not only are they philosophically connected to these street brawlers and murderers; their ideas, if fully implemented, would have the same results today.

After World War II, the progressives tried to regroup but the world had tired of their agitation and for several decades the U.S.A. drifted as a mixed economy, riding the wave of the technological advances made by capitalism during the 19th century culminating today in a generation educated in progressive schools that has no knowledge of the lessons of the 20th century and that is moving headlong into dictatorship without knowing it.

This is partly the result of the progressive agenda which has been a calculated effort to brainwash the younger generation and hide its desire to once again enslave mankind. But it is also partly the result of the fact that capitalism and individual rights has no representative today. Utilizing the tactics of gangsters and racketeers, today's progressives masquerade as "liberals" who say they merely want to "tweak" the economy to make it better, while their actions are actually ushering in a fascist state with most of the characteristics of the Nazis including rabid collectivism, racism and discrimination against businessmen.

There is a clear difference between the ideas of the founders and the ideas of the progressives. The founders were civilized men who crafted a civil society. The progressives were agitators and destroyers of civil society. The founders created the idea of private property. The progressives fought in the streets and destroyed property. The founders made it possible for men to make wealth while the progressives sought to re-distribute (steal) wealth. The founders created a peaceful society while the progressives created a divided society that they made poor through riot and shakedown of property owners. The founders thought about how to protect citizens. The progressives know only thuggery and shakedown. The founders created a society where courts of justice could resolve disputes among citizens. The progressives thought about how to create divisions, polarization, conflict, hatred and discrimination against productive citizens.

With that said, we must learn that reason and man's rights are actually the more advanced set of ideas and that progressivism is a regression into barbarism, exploitation and slavery. We stand on the verge of losing everything our founders built including the intellectual foundations that made our great nation possible. We must, if we are to have a society of justice and prosperity, learn what it means to have a government whose only purpose is to protect individual rights, not violate them.

Properly,

- You have a right to make a living. This means you can create your own job by learning skills and selecting the profession you desire. More than this, you have a right to be proud of making a living. You should never accept the idea that you owe something to a collective or to others. The idea of having a moral obligation to "give back" to society is a collectivist notion intended to make you feel guilty and exploit your production for the sake of despots. The more freedom you have to make a living, the better our society is becoming. Likewise, the more the government creates jobs paid for by the money of other citizens, the worse our society is becoming. You do not have a right to a job created by government for the purpose of giving you an income.
- You have a right to what you create. If you use your mind to create a product, what you create is yours to trade with others or to keep. Your production cannot be taken from you for the sake of a

collective that thinks it knows what to do with your work. In order to be productive, you had to use your mind and, because of this, whatever you produce is yours by right.

- You also have a right to be proud of what you create. You should never accept the idea that all production and creative thought is a collective endeavor undertaken for the sake of the group.
- You have a right to make as much money as you can possibly make. The individual creates wealth and if you have invested time in educating yourself, spent money in buying the tools of production, and worked hard for hour upon hour, the money you make, all of it, should be yours to keep. No one, especially the government, has a right to take it.
- You have a right to say what you think without fear of disapproval from others. Your mind is your property. It is an expression of your excellence and of your ability to ascertain reality. Just as you respect the right of others to think, your right to think should be respected as well. Only when you are free to express what you think are you living in a society that is just and fair. If government assumes the power to tell you how to think and how to express yourself, you are living in a society that considers you a slave. If government attempts to punish you for your ideas, you are living in a dictatorship.
- You have a right to be moral. Whether you are young and inexperienced or old and wise, you are the decision maker about what is right for you. No

one has the authority to dictate to you what you should do. As long as your actions do not violate the rights of others, you have the ability and the obligation to decide for yourself what is moral.

- You have a right to your own philosophy. Whether you accept a religion or a secular philosophy or decide upon your own philosophical views, no one has the right to tell you how you should think. Just as in any other decision, if you accept wrong ideas you will have to deal with the consequences. No one can force you to accept a given religion or body of ideas at the point of a gun or by law.

- You have a right to associate with whomever you like. This right is an extension of the fact that you have a right to decide what is moral. No one has a right to demand that you go to group meetings, that you repeat slogans and that you think group thoughts. You are a free person and you can do as you please so long as you do not violate the rights of others.

- You have a right to all the energy you can use. There is no way you will ever use more energy than is available to the planet. The more energy you use, the more you can produce and the more money you can make. As long as your energy use does not harm the property of others, you should use all the energy you can use to make a better life. Anyone who says you are harming the planet is trying to destroy your mind and stifle your ability to produce, create and enjoy your life.

- You have a right to privacy. What you do in the privacy of your own home is your business so long as you violate no other person's rights. No one has a right to invade your privacy without due process of law whether it is a policeman or a census taker.
- You have a right to your body and your health. Your health decisions are yours to make in consultation with your doctor. The government can never tell you what to do with your body. You have a right to choose your doctor, choose your treatment, choose your method of payment and no one can violate your body and tell you or your doctor what to do.
- You have a right to protect yourself against violence and fraud. The government that seeks to prohibit your right to self-defense is a government intent on robbing you.
- You have a right to live where you want. As long as you are able to trade income for a residence, you are free to live where you choose. No one can tell you what house or what neighborhood should be your abode.
- You have a right to trial by a jury of your peers. A fair trial using objective laws and logical argument is the only way you can keep thieves and government from destroying your rights or stealing your property. It is also the best way to fairly settle disputes among citizens in civil cases.
- You have a right to capital accumulation. Capital accumulation is the method that enables you to grow your wealth. Savings, astutely invested, should never be skimmed by government. When

the government assumes the right to take your savings by means of money inflation or direct taxation, it is operating as a thief. You have the right to keep your savings in whatever form you see fit (such as gold, silver or secured paper). The government has no right to decide for you what currency you should use.

- You have a right to make your own economic decisions. The government has no right to intervene in your economic choices, business operations, banking decisions, transactions or more. It does not have the right to tax your property away or tell you how you should act economically. It has no business regulating your business and as long as you are not defrauding anyone, it should always be "hands off" of your economic activity.

Each of these rights is an extension of the concept of individual rights. If our society respects these rights, then we can have a vibrant, healthy society that is diverse in people and in opinions, where the best ideas win and where there is no limit to how far you can advance. It is a secure society because there are no threats to the individual, where people can trust one another and where self-sufficiency and respect are the hallmarks. Let no one tell you that freedom is the gateway to sin or that self-interest is evil. Never let them tell you that freedom has failed and it is time for central planning. The man who tells you that is a thief. Freedom is the gateway to accomplishment, to cooperation, to reason and to happiness. Anything else is slavery.

The War Against Women and Political Suicide

Senatorial candidate Todd Akin of Missouri committed political suicide in 2012 when he made a very poor choice of words about "forcible rape". However, the uproar against it reeks of political opportunism for both Democrats and Republicans. I think it is very nasty of politicos to raise the "war against women" mantra again and again. For Republicans, Akin gave them an opportunity to throw another Republican under the bus, although he probably deserved it (though he could have been a Trojan horse, bought, paid for and delivered by the Democrats).

I think it is reprehensible to attempt to make political hay out of an issue that is very important and needs to be debated by reasonable people seeking reasonable solutions. Certainly, there is no such thing as "forcible rape". All rape is forcible. That is a fact. But for the left to use this statement to tar and feather all Republicans is unscrupulous and unfair. I would venture to say that few Republicans, if any, favor rape.

Keep in mind, I'm not a big defender of Republicans and have done my share of ridiculing them. But the idea that there is a war on women does a disservice to the women who have been raped and it unfairly tarnishes the reputations of the many Republicans who also care about women who have been raped. Democrats are no more for women or against them than are Republicans. According to this faulty logic, you could equally say that Democrats have a war on women because so many women have lost their jobs since Obama has been President.

The mistake here is the practice of invoking collectivism; the grouping of people, in this case, according to ideas that many of them do not hold. There are many women Republicans who don't feel they are at war with women. Some Republican women, a few, even favor a woman's right to abortion. In fact, they think that free market principles and policies are the best way to help women as well as men (and blacks and gays). Many Republicans believe that you don't help people by expropriating money from one group, and then using that money in wasteful and even harmful ways presumably to help another group...such as paying approximately $1,000,000 per job created – most of which jobs do not return the "investment" (like jobs are supposed to do). It doesn't take a Republican to adhere to sound economic principles; it takes a sound thinker adhering to individual rights. In fact, this wasteful spending could be said to represent a war by the Democrats on the entire country.

Regarding tax payers paying for abortions or the consequences of rape, I first would like to state that I am in favor of a woman's right to do whatever she and her doctor decide is in her best interests. I fully support a woman's right to control her body and to make all decisions without the interference of government (or men). I consider the idea of outlawing abortions to be a violation of the woman's individual rights. On this point, I disagree with many of my Republican friends who have a different view of the good and how it is derived.

However, I do not support the idea that government should use tax payer dollars to fund abortions. I consider it immoral to force one individual to pay for the needs of any other individual. If I want to help women get abortions, I should support that privately with private donations and not ask the government to do it. Using tax payer dollars to pay for abortions, houses, solar panels, cars, factories and windmills, etc. is wrong.

The key question to ask in this context is "what is the proper role of government?" I hold that each individual is properly responsible for him or herself and I consider it evil to demand that other people pay for anyone else's stuff. Government should not be a provider of benefits that are paid for by the tax payer. It should be a protector of individual rights; a defender of people against having their right to life and property violated.

The fact that I don't support the right of a person to take my money and give it to someone else does not mean I am at war against women. Welfare and welfare services, or any government services (even those that support big corporations and thieving CEOs), are not a right. No person has a right to demand that other people lose their rights in order to pay for someone else's "rights". To insist that it is proper to take other peoples' money by force is wrong – yet that is what the leftists (and some on the right) do. This violation of individual rights is what many progressive advocates of abortion are demanding. They are demanding that government, meaning the tax payer, pay for abortions and contraception. They have a right to abortions and contraception if they want to purchase them...but they don't have a right to force other people to pay for them.

But I consider the issue of funding abortions to be part of a larger struggle for freedom. People should be free to use their hard earned money as they see fit - and that right is more important than anyone else's need because it provides the means by which people solve their own problems - morally.

The real issue in any modern election should be individual rights. The issue of funding abortions is an important part of that debate but it is only part of the wider debate. Most of us are aware that once the present crop of Democrats is done implementing their re-distribution policies, if we elect them again, there eventually won't be any money for anything...and that includes money for abortions and rape victims. If we become insolvent as a country, there won't be any benefits for anyone, seniors, women or government cronies. There won't be any money to scream about and demand (as a right) because the Democrats will have forced us into bankruptcy...and bankruptcy means there is no more money.

Supporting the Democrats and their spending, even their spending on abortion, will not make things better...it will eventually cause the financial and economic collapse of our country. That would cause a real war on women and men and children and Blacks and Hispanics and anyone. If you want our country to collapse, vote for the Democrats.

If you want it to collapse a few months later, vote for mainstream Republicans.

The Conservative's Dilemma

In spite of everything I've written here, the idea that leftists and rightists are morally equivalent is not true anymore. We are no longer in a situation where the left merely wants to extend the American dream to more people. Today, the left has become oppressive and harmful. In fact, the left has become a bastion of hatred of capitalism and even of a desire to vilify and punish successful individuals. We are fast approaching a situation where the rich are considered so evil that, in the not too distant future, harsher treatment may be in store for them. The vandalism of throwing rocks at their nice cars will turn to riots and violence as well as more onerous taxes and regulations, jailings and persecution – as part of leftist government policy.

The left uses the concept of the "social contract" to create a group of "takers" who proclaim that they have been given, by the people, the responsibility for re-distributing wealth. They are oblivious to the idea that in our system, the majority is not supposed to have the right to dispose of the minority. This exposes the lie of the left; the social contract is not a contract at all but a convenient device that enables the left to circumvent individual rights and to take the peoples' property under the guise of doing the will of the people.

The takers are made up of people who have no problem making cavalier decisions about the rights and properties of individuals. They may speak of a hopeful future but that is window dressing. Nothing stops them from drawing up regulations or edicts that force people to do their bidding. When the left speaks, it is as if no one has any rights and anyone who would oppose "social justice" is an ignorant, uneducated "yokel" who should just shut up. Their idea of enlightened government is best exemplified by the issuance of arbitrary commands that must be followed - or else. Although they pander to ignorance if it benefits them, they have no regard whatsoever for private individuals whose taxes must pay for their grand ideas and cronyism.

But this is where conservatives fall apart. They pretend to oppose the left but never oppose the basic premises of the left. When a leftist politician proposes a new tax, the conservatives are quick to say, "Yes, but…" Rather than defending the individual rights of the taxpayer. Instead, they claim that the best way to get more of the taxpayer's money is to lower taxes. So, even for the conservatives, the taxpayer is superfluous. He has no defender of his rights. The conservatives are opponents who do not oppose.

The coercive activities of the left have created a backlash among people whose money is being taken. These are the "makers" who understand that there is no "social contract" that gives anyone a right to dispose of their lives, income and property. The makers have educated themselves about the original intent of the Constitution and they seek to re-establish the right to live freely. Whether you call them Tea Party or independents, they have learned that their only proper obligation to others is to respect their individual rights. The makers present no demand for the confiscation of money from the rich. They not only defend the rich but they defend their own right to make money and keep it. Not all of them want to do away with taxes but many of them want to do away with the IRS.

These shifts of focus away from principles by the conservatives have brought us to a critical point as a nation. Do we stand on principle or do we give in to fear of the opinions of progressives? The progressives will not relent in their demands for sacrifice, re-distribution and helping the poor. They will not give up and there is no one to stand against them; no one willing to challenge self-sacrifice as morality.

This is indeed, the Conservative's dilemma. Conservatives are being led by a group that thinks it is their responsibility to compromise with the progressives rather than oppose them. Conservative politicians will run for election as opposition candidates but after they are elected, they oppose no one. Indeed, one must wonder if conservative mainstream politicians are a Trojan Horse hiding their true progressivism.

It is certainly true that neocons want to beat the progressives to their own game by out spending them. They seem to think that the tide of political winds is with the progressives so there is no point in opposing their violations of our liberties. This is why President Obama got everything he wanted and why the conservatives were timid and mealy mouthed in opposing his demands.

Today, many Americans realize that so much is on the line that someone must take a stand for freedom. This requires opposing "legal" theft by government. This requires understanding that there is no moral equivalency between a thief and an honest person or between collectivism and freedom. You cannot have a little bit of total sacrifice; just as you cannot choose to be a little bit moral. As Dr. Tara Smith observes, "If individuals *owe* one another their services, they can be licensed no freedom to shirk that obligation."[27]

Because collectivism is an immoral idea, it is imperative that we be uncompromising when it comes to defending freedom. As individuals, we must do everything possible to block collectivists from using government power to advance their goals. There is no compromise possible with people who insist that government can do whatever it wishes to people. Granting such a premise will destroy us as it has destroyed many societies in the past.

Progressives are more than willing to compromise on the amount and level of progressive theft. Once you compromise on those premises they win every time. They tell you they want to "do good" but their only power is that you think they are doing good. What if they are not doing good?

---

[27] Moral Rights and Political Freedom, Dr. Tara Smith, Rowman and Littlefield Publishers, Inc. Page 78

Collectivism, as it is preached by the progressives, means the sacrifice of some for the sake of the few. It means enslavement, imprisonment and the destruction of man's mind. It demands conformity and submission from the individual and it will not rest until it has destroyed the best among us.

We don't need to get along with collectivists; we need an open fight with them (a political debate about principles) and we must win that fight with better, more rational and more practical ideas. We must block them at every turn and we must convince people that the best way to have a good life is to live free of government coercion.

A political debate about principles must truly be about principles and this is where the conservatives today fall short. This is where they must come to grips with the principles that our society needs if we are to avoid the collectivist steamroller.

If you adhere to individual rights, you must adhere to the right of a woman to control her body, not to the right of the government to control her decisions and actions. You must believe in the rights of honest immigrants to leave oppressive nations so they can live in freedom (while adding their productive abilities to one of the most productive societies in history). You must believe in the right of every American to keep what he earns and do what he wants with his earnings. If you believe in individual rights there is no "freedom of speech *but...*". You must defend the right to own a gun without registering it as well as the right to make your own economic decisions without government regulations. You must fight for the rights of atheists *not* to believe and to live free of the imposition of religion into the public (governmental) arena.

Ask virtually any conservative today and he will give you a long litany of reasons why people should not enjoy full freedom, why some people are not deserving of the right to live as they see fit. You will hear that women want to kill babies, immigrants want to gain welfare, millionaires should provide a "safety net", the productive should pay a ransom in taxes and that freedom of speech should not be offensive, that gun rights require registration, that a little bailout here and there is not such a bad thing and that anyone who does not believe in God is trying to destroy "American values" and turn us into a communist dictatorship. All such arguments make conservatives the allies of progressives.

You can't advocate for individual rights "*but*" and still consider yourself a consistent advocate of individual rights. Just like those Americans who advocate freedom of speech "*but*" and immigration "*but*"[28] and a woman's right "*but*" or a businessman's rights "*but*", you would be fighting for eventual enslavement.

And since the progressives are consistent advocates of government force, since they believe that man is fallible

---

[28] I am for open immigration made available to people who have been vetted as honest, hardworking and disease-free.

and weak; that he must be forced to be moral; there is no way you can fight for freedom without being FOR freedom and everything that entails.

Who has the Courage?

I have been appalled at the low level of intellect, understanding, forthrightness and principle of political candidates who, for some reason, believe they have the qualifications to lead the greatest country in history. I am further appalled at the low level of judgment that has characterized the voters who have given these men and women leadership positions. With that said, I am wondering if there is a man or woman on the scene who has the courage to run a political campaign based on the following:

Individual rights

The Constitution establishes the right of the individual to be free of government coercion. It sets the rules for how the government should operate by establishing freedom of religion as well as freedom from religion, freedom of speech, freedom of association, freedom from unreasonable search and seizure, right to bear arms, property rights, the pursuit of happiness and much more.

Is there a candidate who would reinstitute individual rights by establishing several policy positions. These include:

Policy 1. Transition our government through three stages to eliminate the IRS.
Stage 1. Move to a temporary National Sales Tax.
Stage 2. Gradually eliminate all government programs based upon re-distribution of income from one group to

another. These include welfare programs, jobs programs, housing programs, Medicare and Medicaid and Social Security to name a few. Where possible, privatize these programs gradually. Ensure that all people who are legally vested in these programs receive their full benefits but allow no new payees into the programs.
Stage 3. Totally eliminate the IRS, the National Sales Tax and set up a system of voluntary support of government services as well as direct payments (use charges) for services such as courts, contract enforcement, etc.

Policy 2. Create a Constitutional Amendment to eliminate government interference in the economy. Until such an amendment can be ratified, it will be the policy of the new administration to eliminate all government interference in the economy including the dismantling of every regulatory agency of the Federal government.

Policy 3. Eliminate the Federal Reserve Bank and immediately return to the gold standard.

Foreign Policy

Policy 1. Immediately declare America's goal to eliminate any foreign threat that is presently engaged in military action against America or American interests abroad. This policy will not seek to win "hearts and minds" but to eliminate any threat as soon as possible by whatever means necessary - once the threat is eliminated, we will leave.

Policy 2. Announce a unilateral elimination of any trade barriers that are presently in place by the U.S. government. U.S. citizens can decide individually or corporately which nations they will choose for trade. The only exception would be nations that have sworn to destroy the U.S. or any U.S. allies.

Policy 3. Remove the U.S. as a member of the United Nations and politely ask the UN to move its headquarters to another country within 2 years.

Policy 4. Immediately convene a commission to reform immigration laws and policies so our country can attract an adequate number of hard working immigrants seeking freedom and prosperity. Key goals of this commission will be to ensure an adequate level of immigration that will fill the demand for new workers; ensure that every immigrant is treated with respect; vet every immigrant to ensure he or she is law-abiding, honest, and free of contagious disease; reform the system so it does not unfairly restrict immigration; implement the Constitutional principle that "all men are created equal" and finally; ensure that immigrants do not come here for a government "hand-out."

Education

Policy 1. Eliminate the U.S Department of Education.

Policy 2. Place all schools owned by the Federal Government up for sale to the highest bidder.

Policy 3. Eliminate the laws that mandate that any child in the U.S. must attend school as a matter of law.

Once elected, this new President could use this Inauguration Speech:

My fellow Americans, we stand today in a time that has seen the most serious decline of the power and prestige of our country in its history. The causes of this decline are many but it goes without saying that the fundamental cause is government intervention in our economy and most importantly interference into the private lives and decisions of our citizens. We have seen the damage done by runaway government. The myth of government power has blinded us about the very real damage that can be done by government to the free choices and business decisions of our citizens.

I declare that the human mind must be free to function and any individual who works hard and produces abundance must be free to keep that abundance and enjoy his or her life. The long nightmare of worshipping the power of government is over. The people have their lives back and the government will soon get out of their way.

My administration will return our nation to the root principles that created it – the very principles that made it great. For the first time in many years, you will have a leader who believes that principles matter. What are these principles that will guide my administration?

For decades, we have been taught that statism and interventionism were the way for government to ensure a more equitable society. It was thought for many years that a capitalist system inevitably left some people behind and that the rich got richer.

Yet, history proved that a free society lifted up poor people and gave them better life styles than those of kings of old. No one noticed that the technology advances brought by capitalist innovators were being enjoyed by both rich and poor.

Yet throughout this period, the call was for more regulation, higher taxes and more government intrusions into our every-day decisions. These recommendations were accompanied by the imposition of a national income tax, massive government programs and deficit spending, all supported by massive government-funded propaganda campaigns against capitalism and a takeover of the schools that were supposed to educate our children.

An even worse spectacle were the long lines of private businesses that sought government money to save their businesses, help with cash flow or finance huge boondoggles. This practice will stop today, not next year, not in the unforeseeable future. No one can obtain money from the government in the form of welfare or loans.

I declare a policy of immediate elimination of all government intervention into the economy. This will eliminate the need for career politicians; it will eliminate the need for campaign contributions and there will be no need for quid pro quo or bribery. Finally, politicians will be required to do their jobs which is to protect individual rights rather than countenance their violation.

The worst principle that a free society can accept is the idea that the government has the right to re-distribute money from one citizen to another. It is this principle that has destroyed countless nations and caused monumental disasters even in our own country.

Regarding the education of our young people, my administration will do away with government-run schools; further, it will fight for a school system that is free of government control. Parents will now be able to choose which schools their children will attend, which curricula and subjects will be taught and they will never be forced again to accept the imposition of ideas with which they disagree. Further, I will abolish the monopoly that teachers unions have in our schools by eliminating the requirement that teachers must join a union. If we are to have a free society, your schools must be free of government or control by government supported labor unions. This includes our universities, colleges and technical schools.

As a society that was founded upon individual rights and freedom, we have learned the value of a Constitutional government that is restricted to protecting the rights of citizens; a government whose purpose is to defend those rights rather than violate them. I pledge to you that individual rights will not be mere political rhetoric in my administration; these words will not be empty; they will be the principles that guide us. If it is a crime for a citizen to rob another citizen, it is a crime for the government to do the same.

Likewise, as a free nation, we prefer to deal economically and diplomatically first with those countries that have similar free societies and individual protections. We pledge to those countries an abiding friendship and open trade. As with domestic economic policy, we pledge a "hands off" foreign economic policy.

But we also know that our country has enemies who want to harm or destroy us. Dictatorships and terrorist groups that have no regard for the lives and property of their fellow citizens pose a threat to their neighbors and to the world. Many try to justify their hatred of us by accusing us of brutal acts or of seeking to dominate the world. Their arguments are based upon lies and prejudice. Let me state clearly that the United States of America holds by conviction that "all men are created equal" and this applies to men of other nations. If you want to be our friend, we welcome you with open arms. If you want to do us harm, we will ensure that you spend your time hiding, starving or dying.

We pledge our Armed Forces and Intelligence Services to be always vigilant to the activities of our enemies and we will do whatever is necessary to thwart them before they can accomplish their destructive aims.

Finally, my fellow Americans, I want to make it clear that we need an Amendment to our Constitution that strictly prohibits government interference in the economy. Just as we have a separation of church and state in our Constitution, true freedom requires a separation of economy and state. There has never been a situation in our history where our government's interventions into the economy have served a useful purpose. This ability of the government to regulate and control the economy has resulted in the impoverishment of our people and this must be stopped. The only way to stop the corruption and theft that government interference has brought about is to prohibit the government from making any regulations that interfere or regulate economic activity. Since this issue has been the keynote of my candidacy, I thank you for your support and I promise that we will begin immediately to remove the corruption of government from our lives and daily decisions.

My fellow Americans, I am not going to ask you to sacrifice. I am not going to ask you for more of your money; nor will I slyly advance massive spending programs while I promise to cut spending. Those of you who have listened to inaugural addresses in the past are accustomed to hearing clever phrases demanding collective solutions for individual problems. Today is a new day and I won't ask you to marvel and my clever eloquence. I am going to provide you with one of the most quotable lines ever to be uttered. "We hold these truths to be self-evident, that all men are created equal, that they are endowed by their Creator with certain unalienable Rights, that among these are Life, Liberty and the pursuit of Happiness."

Thank you for your support.

Who has the courage?

Other books by Robert Villegas

The Age of Selfishness
Behind the Ritual Mask
The Battle of the Sexes
Individualism
Crushing the Alinsky Radicals
Bob and Bobbie
The Raven Haired Girl
The Boy who Stood Alone
Adam Reborn
Adam Reborn and Adam Rayberne
Poetic Prose and Poetry
Poems for the Stage – A Story of Love
Poems for the Stage – The Man at the Computer
Unkilling Jesus
Finding Sponsors
Finding Sponsors 2
The Hospitality Event Planning Handbook
The Sport Sponsor Handbook
How to Write a Sponsorship Proposal
Website Development Methodology

To Order go to

www.robertvillegas.com

Twitter: @RobertVillega18

Facebook: Robert Villegas

About Robert Villegas

Robert Villegas is an Indiana Author specializing in fiction, romance, theater, politics and philosophy. He was born in South Texas (Weslaco) but raised in Indiana. He is Hispanic-American but American in every sense of the word. He has spent a lifetime in the business world as a UPS executive and also worked in locations all over the United States and Europe. He is an Army veteran who served in Korea as a telecommunications specialist serving in the 7th Infantry Division in Camp Casey, Korea. He was educated in Indiana and earned a Degree through the University of the State of NY (Albany) via an external degree program. He is divorced with three grown children and three grandchildren.

Mr. Villegas is a student of the philosophy of Objectivism authored by Ayn Rand. However, he is not a spokesperson for the philosophy. His ideas are from his own personal experience and study and are his sole responsibility.

www.ingramcontent.com/pod-product-compliance
Lightning Source LLC
Chambersburg PA
CBHW070104300526
45788CB00016B/2267